Magical Essence of Being:
Human & Divine

My life's path has merged, parted, and reconnected with Jeanie's for the past 30 years. During this time, Jeanie has been a creative, intelligent, and loving presence in my life. I am pleased to be witness to her high energy and the completion of this inspiring book. Enjoy traveling with her, just as I have.

—Jan O'Mara, San Luis Obispo CA

So many beings on the Planet are now in service to humanity, yet few serve with ALL they are, with as much Wisdom, Compassion, and Enthusiasm as Jeanie Lemaire. She brings life to "Being" human in an enormous, completely individual, and authentic way. She totally supports each person she works with in re-claiming their true Self, and in being 100% loving, real, and here. Her metaphors are delightful and insightful, aiding us in seeing ourselves with more gentleness and levity. Jeanie came into my life in 1983 as a great lift and continues to marvel, encourage, and inspire me.

—Eda Nell Long, Dallas TX

I could go on and on about what a special person Jeanie is and the influence she has had on my life, but the point is, I was so fascinated with the interconnectedness of the whole being—which Jeanie helped bring into my awareness—that I enrolled in a massage training course. I am now a Certified Massage Therapist and offer my clients an opportunity to share their quests and growth with me. If I can in some small way be of assistance to others as Jeanie was/is to me, I will feel I am contributing to the shift in awareness that is now occurring.

—Skye Patterson, Los Osos CA

Magical Essence of Being:
Human & Divine

Imagenetics™ and Humanology in Motion™

by

Jeanie Lemaire

Co-written with

Corinn Codye

Artwork by

Rachel Harwell

**Balancing
Arts**

info@jeanielemaire.com
(909) 835-3137
www.jeanielemaire.com

ISBN 0-9648540-1-5

Library of Congress Catalog Card Number: 98-071299

Published by Balancing Arts
P.O. Box 2873
Wrightwood, California 92397-2873
Telephone: (760) 249-3343

Printed in the United States of America.

99 00 01 02 03 04 05 06 07 08

10 9 8 7 6 5 4 3 2 1

The paper used in this publication meets the minimum requirements of the American National Standard for Permanence of Paper for Printed Library Materials Z39.48-1984.

♡

Dedication

I lovingly dedicate this book to **Corinn Codye** and **Rachel Harwell**—
two beautiful Beings, whose huge hearts and creative skills,
along with their **Unicorn** and **Elvian** Essences,
have made this book a joy-filled reality.

♡

Joy & Delight !

Jeanie

♡ ♡ ♡

Nothing's more important than the Oneness space,
It comes from your heart, it's a Happy place.
Love can put a smile on your face,
And gives you so much more.

—from *The Oneness Space*

♡ ♡ ♡

♡ TABLE OF CONTENTS ♡

♡ PREFACE ♡

Many people have asked me, after reading the first book, *The Body Talks...and I Can Hear It*, which deals with bringing the three "dense" systems or means of communicating the Self (physical, mental, and emotional) into balance, why it is that I forgot to include the spiritual body. For, after all, isn't that the whole point of exploring the Self—to find that spiritual part of our Self and integrate it into our daily living?

I, in my usual "unusual" humor, could only chuckle, because for so long, some of us weren't even aware that we had a spiritual aspect in us. However, in actuality, this Self or essence that I keep alluding to—which appears as "The Being" in these books, and which is not our physical form or our thoughts or our feelings, but rather expresses through these three levels—*is* the eternal spiritual factor that we are. The "spiritual being" is not something we acquire or regain, for it is never gone—just sometimes misplaced, ignored, or denied.

Indeed, once we let go of poor self-esteem, ignorance, and loss, we quite naturally pop right back into our Self as a consciously connected expression of love, joy, support, balance, enthusiasm, happiness, and so on. Now tell me anyone who isn't interested in these traits. If they say they are not, then look for poor self-esteem, which shows up in some as anger and in others as victimhood, unworthiness, or fatigue. Or look for ignorance, which shows up in some as uninterest and in others as negative judgment, impatience, aggression, or denial—as in "not wanting those things" or as explanations and defense.

In any event, the days when we humans actually thought we were fooling others by keeping our thoughts to ourselves, by keeping ourselves "separate" from the whole, or by saying one thing and doing another, are just about over. And, the shift toward awareness of our connectedness is part of the panic in those who have had to defend themselves and their ideas for so long that they no longer remember how to cooperate or interrelate. Panic is also very evident in those who have been so repeatedly attacked— physically, mentally, emotionally, spiritually, or on all levels—that to get them to relax, be vulnerable, and let love in, is next to impossible, because one more betrayal will break their hearts just too many times.

In this work, including our notions of *Imagenetics*™ and *Humanology in Motion*™, we aim to address not only the panic, disorientation, and sense of separation, but also to help ease the shift in awareness toward Totality and connectedness. By all this, Corinn and I hope to provide a means of initiating and extending an experiential conversation, through which we can examine ourselves, the world around us, and what it means to be a Human and Divine Being—playfully of course.

Humanology in Motion™ refers to the study of humans, that is, *not* their history, socialization, or actions, but rather the inner meaning of what it is to *be* human. I've finally come to the realization that despite all other titles, certificates, and degrees, the title that most accurately describes me is *Humanologist and Practitioner of the Invisible Arts*. This announces that I am primarily concerned with the spiritual awareness or "Being" that lives inside a human skin-suit and under the jurisdiction of human laws. Therefore, the most important task of *Humanology in Motion*™ is to "link up" the eternal Self with the current human expression of that Self.

"And just what are the *invisible arts*?" you might ask. To me, they have to do with exploring our invisible or cosmic aspects. For a very long time, we humans have invested tremendous energy into our mental and technological development, or aspects outside of the Self. Actually, I for one am pleased that someone has been interested enough to pursue such goals, because it has provided us with many wonderful conveniences, such as indoor plumbing and countless other aids to daily living. It's just that *my* focus is on an equally important facet of the human nature and experi-ence—that of our *connection* to ourselves, each other, and all of Life. Unfortunately, this critical part of our sense of Self, *i.e.,* as a valuable part of the whole, cannot be graded or measured in an academic way, for it is *invisible*. So, not surprisingly, the *invisible arts*, as such, are not currently developed in the school systems, which tend to focus on mental develop-ment.

The key word in **Humanology** and the invisible arts is *experiential*. For in any given moment, our physical forms and feelings *know* our truth. For example, meditation and stillness are invisible arts, and they tap that place of *experience* where Truth is a given, where Love is a given, and where Happiness is a given. Another invisible art is that of listening for what isn't said in words, which some may call mental telepathy, but I call it *knowingness*—accessing All Knowledge or the Akashic records.

Imagenetics, for its part, has to do with the means by which *magic* or *imagination* perpetuates itself through humans. In other words, *magic* or *imagination* is the *invisible* part of our consciousness, and its *visible* counterpart is *nature*. *Imagenetics*, then, deals with how this invisible aspect survives through six **Magical Essences** or viewing places on Totality: the **Angelic**, **Fairy**, **Elvian**, **Unicorn**, **Dwarvian**, and **Wizard**.

Magical Essence of Being builds on the foundation of our previous book, *The Body Talks...and I Can Hear It*, where we deal with clearing and aligning the three densest systems through which the eternal Self ex-presses in third-dimensional living. Here, we focus on the "eternal factor" itself, not only by introducing the six Magical Essences that express through us, as us, but also by exploring the two communication doorways through which each of these Essences express, making twelve perceptual viewing places in all. Also in our sequel, the three densest means of human expression (the physical, mental, and emotional bodies) meet up with their expanded versions, all of which express our "eternal factor" in the invisible realms.

Having studied humans for almost thirty years, I've discovered that there are no "pat" answers—only choices. I have made a number of choices in my life, and no one can tell me whether they were right or wrong for me, except me. As I see it, no human knows exactly where fate and destiny leave off and free will begins. So for me, life is more of a blueprint from which we set out on a journey into the mysteries of consciousness than a play that is "set" in all its circumstances, and the journey itself may carry the key, rather than the goal or end result.

One thing is for sure. No matter how many past lives we have had, no matter what planet we have come from, no matter what mystery school we have attended, no matter how close we are to the masters—here on planet Earth, if we are in a human skin-suit, we are under the jurisdiction of human laws. And that is our greatest challenge, each of us—to take what we know from the Akashic records and our own intuitive awareness and to show up here in the physical world in integrity, with our words and actions matching. Otherwise put, when *verbal understanding* (in the mental body) meets up with heartfelt *knowingness* (in the emotional body), the result is universal *compassion* (in physical actions)—and we experience a state of *connectedness*—human and divine.

This compassion and connectedness reflects the recognition of a greater power or larger picture than any one human can hold, which is why more and more people are awakening to the beautifully orchestrated and synchronized flow of the Universe. We are not here to push another's river or forcibly change the direction of its flow, but rather to own and operate our individual perceptions and contributions to this greater whole, simply by following our heart's desire and our creative passions. Once we come "on line" within our Self, then our integrity, acceptance, and gratitude in daily life becomes a "living example" for others, who can then choose these values for themselves or not. In either event, the tidal ebb and flow of the ocean known as Universal Synchronicity, into which all rivers flow, continues on its journey, undisturbed by humanity's droughts, raging rivers, or flooded areas. Thus, we open a doorway or conversation along the human quest to grasp the never-ending quality of eternity within the confines of an individual Life—which is the truly priceless gift that we all can offer each other.

—Jeanie Lemaire
April 1998

*When I examine myself and my methods of thought,
I come to the conclusion that the gift of fantasy has meant
more to me than my talent for absorbing positive knowledge.*
—Albert Einstein

*Personally, I feel it is not how much knowledge you have that is
important, but how your knowledge helps and improves your life.*
—Michael Tse, *Qigong for Health & Vitality*

*Until he extends his circle of compassion to all living things,
man will not himself find peace.*
—Albert Schweitzer

*… And we are all connected to each other
In a circle, in a hoop that never ends.*
—Stephen Schwartz, "Colors of the Wind,"
Disney's *Pocahontas*

♡ ACKNOWLEDGMENTS ♡

Having written one book and now finishing another, I can better understand why honorees at the academy awards for motion pictures thank so many people for influencing their accomplished feat. I immediately wish to thank Corinn Codye and Rachel Harwell for bringing these invisible awarenesses into thought and form. Corinn not only organized my many tiny scraps of paper with scribbled thoughts into an orderly fashion, she immersed her Self into its principles and *became* the project, thereby providing a support much grander than her many skills. And thanks to Rachel and her ability to take random invisible notions and transform them into artwork that clearly "gets" the gist of my vagueness: such a gift is a wonder to me. There literally would not be a book without these two extraordinarily talented and delightful people. So, I want to say *thank you* for your wonderful contributions to both books and to me, in support, in suggestions, and in loving connection as lifelong friends.

Another huge thank you goes to Paul and Nancy Clemens and all the staff at Blue Dolphin Publishing, for all their assistance in getting both this and the previous book printed, including Lito Castro's capable help on cover layout, Linda Maxwell's impeccable skills in text setting and page design, and John Mello's and Jill Sonnenberg's assistance in smoothing the flow of production.

In addition, I want to thank my family, my friends, and my clients for allowing me that rare privilege of knowing you on the inside, and for experiencing you all as one and the same to me—loving connections. A special thanks to Debbie Miller, Cliff Lardinois, Ginny Fereira, Rich Juarez, Jennifer Snouffer, Patty Conte, Tom White, Robin Fennell, Dan

Gardner, and Theresa Marie, for their generous hearts, both financially and unconditionally.

For those who know me and know that I consider everything to be "alive" as vibrating energy—I also wish to thank my three cars over the last 20 years, *Strider the Silver Streak* (Mazda GLC), *Chez-san* (Honda Civic), and *Chrystara* (Saturn wagon), for taking such good care of me during my many wanderings back and forth between the east and west coasts of the U.S. And absolutely very dear to my heart, to the two most special dogs in my life—from childhood, *Ella*, and as an adult, *Gabriella*—I give a great big thanks for always being there for me with unconditional love and support.

Lastly, and definitely not at the end but truly the beginning of my gratitude, I thank the Universe, or God, or Totality, or my larger Self, for the awesome experience of being in form at such a tremendous time in Earth history.

♡ INTRODUCTION ♡

If you asked most folks how the world works, you might hear, "It's a dog-eat-dog world out there," or, "People just are not friendly." Or, "If you want a decent retirement lifestyle, you'd better get started now (when you are young), or it will never happen."

If you listen closely, all these phrases imply that you can't count on anyone but yourself. The language seems in fact to assume that we are all separate entities, with each of us having to reinvent the wheel of life, on our own, and that, if we do a good job (*i.e.,* get plenty of money and things), then we become a successful human being.

Well, *what if,* just maybe, everyone is not really as separate as we appear and we are actually directly connected to everyone and everything. What if this separate-appearing self is really a chunk or section of a larger Self, known to us as "all of the Universe" or "Oneness." And what if each individual person, place, or thing is actually part of us in a very real way— even though we have forgotten this truth, simply because most of us are not visibly joined at the hip.

This exact shift in *invisible* perception has the potential to transform life as we know it, for how we "hold" situations and interactions literally "colors" our view of them, and ultimately this affects how we interact with others.

As a matter of fact, such a shift *is* taking place, for have you noticed that phrases such as, *Oh, isn't that a shame!* or *Isn't it awful...!* (as though nothing could be done about whatever it is) are passing out of vogue and are actually used less and less often these days. To us, this trend indicates that this very shift in perception—of how we hold ourselves in relation to our-Selves and other-Selves—is truly well underway. That is, we are now beginning to consciously choose whether to struggle along the way, like weary salmon swimming upstream to reach the spot where we finally die, or to go happily with the flow in a swift and easy journey. In this shift comes the realization that our focus need not leave our own "back yard," but that instead we can give everyone the freedom to explore their own path and learn the lessons they set out to "get" while in human form—as opposed to imposing *our* version of what their lessons should be or our judgment as to their progress.

So—given that such a shift *is* in fact underway:

What if you could "know" a person, just by listening to their enthusiasm and "energy"?

What if you could be better heard and received in your communication?

What if the Universe, as known to us at this time, is not only perfectly orchestrated in its alignment of planets, stars, moons, and suns, but also a mirror reflection of the perfection in each of us, as Beings, while we are in human "skin-suits" here on planet Earth?

What if the answers to our daily concerns are being sent to us all the time, through cosmic grandeur?

What if, crazy as it may seem, each of us is a mini-representation of the greater Universe at large?

*And, what if those "two" universes—the individual self and the greater Self—could meet and operate as **one**?*

This book, the second of two that have been asked to be present on the planet at this time, is the story of these possibilities. It links the emotional, mental, and physical components of ourselves to total spiritual awareness, or Being-ness. This eternal spiritual quality is not separate from us or from

Oneness; however, for purposes of exploration, we are going to view "it" as a number of perceptual viewing places, which we call the *Magical Essences.*

The information on people's Magical Essences—the **Angelic, Fairy, Elvian, Unicorn, Dwarvian,** or **Wizard**—began with a notion seeded in Jeanie's subconscious mind that gradually worked its way to the surface of conscious possibility. It's hard to say when the awareness first gelled into an idea, for her work over the past thirty years has, like most folks', continued to expand. However, at some point during the past decade the notion dawned that not only do we humans approach this life through either a "mental" or an "emotional" base of communication,[1] but also that within each of us is a "viewing place" on Totality, a viewing place that has been with each of us since long before form, time, or space became a factor. This viewing place is invisible yet "get-able" and is discussed here in magical terms.

Having no "form," the **Magical Essences** emerged as a way to give safety to Jeanie's body therapy clients during her process of merging with them in consciousness—resulting in clearings and cleansings, physically, mentally, and emotionally, all at the same time. This process holographically and profoundly affects her clients' views of their "perceptual niches" in life—in a way that does not threaten or contradict their belief systems, religions, or philosophies. By linking people up with their **Magical Essences**, she provides an *experiential bridge* between people's daily concerns and their intrinsic Incredible Magnificent Priceless nature.

It is her contention that in Earth terms an original dichotomy exists between Magic and Nature, and that over the eons of time and timelessness, these two realms coexisted and were both visible until humanity grew so out-of-whack or out-of-touch that the magical realms simply

---

[1] These "bases" and their interactions are introduced in *The Body Talks...and I Can Hear It.*

became invisible. Yet, just maybe the **Magical Essences** have survived not just as stories and entertainment and a slender thread of history, but as humanity itself. In other words, what if, just maybe, the **Magical Essences** are actually alive here and now, expressing their cosmic "viewing points"—all of which originated at or before the moment of creation, surviving eternally, and expressing through all humans, *as us*, whether we are aware of this factor or not?

In this light, we have woven these ideas of the interface between the visible and the invisible realms, of the greater Self and the individual Self, of the seemingly random and the perfectly orchestrated, into something that can be grasped and discussed.

The actual gathering of information for this "cosmic conversation" took place through the opportunity to work and interact personally with large numbers of people across the country in Jeanie's body integration therapy practice. Over time, the **Magical Essences** made their presence increasingly "knowable," and the gathered data amassed itself into what we now call *Humanology in Motion*™, or the work of being able to link up the cosmic or eternal "Self" with the current human expression of that Self, and *Imagenetics*™, or the understanding of how magic (the invisible realm) survives and evolves itself via humanity.

The link-up of this cosmic dichotomy is *Being: Human and Divine,* for at any given moment, each of us is both a complete aspect of the whole as well as an individual expression of that wholeness, simply by being present. All the information herein is designed to help reawaken the "knowingness" that although we appear separate (and sometimes isolated and alone), in truth we are all connected, and that just maybe the shift in this perception is what our collective presence is all about at this time on planet Earth. By purposefully stirring up a conversation on these notions—a conversation that we foresee with great optimism may become obsolete in our own lifetimes—perhaps we can encourage humans to move more fully into their awareness of connectedness, as well as into their acceptance and gratitude for all points of view and lifestyles.

So, without further ado, prepare your Self to take a magical journey into the realms of pure perception, setting aside for the time being "that which you know to be true," and opening your inner doors to mystical magical wonder, dreams, and possibilities. Who knows, the **Magical Essence** you find along the way might just be your Self. So, rest easy and don't work too hard at "getting" this information, for a key factor prevalent in each of the **Magical Essences** is a natural desire to explore the world through play.

At the outset, we remind you that there are no right or wrong approaches to the Self, nor any one way to do, know, or experience the Self, and this endeavor is not so much about providing set answers as about generating individual questions, as in, *Just exactly who and what are we?*, according to our life circumstances, as we perceive them. Perhaps together, dear reader, we may create a greater understanding of the world in which we live.

The nicest part about this whole journey is that there are no exams to pass, no positions to defend, no race to win, and literally no one to impress. At the risk of repeating ourselves, as expressed in *The Body Talks...and I Can Hear It*: **You are, always have been, and always will be a Magnificent Incredible Priceless Gift—just in "being" you,** and it is our hope that no matter what detour you feel you might have taken from the main road of life, that you may recognize here that *All Roads Lead to Home*, Home to the Human and Divine Self that we all are.

...the Fantastic, for us, is not imaginary.
But an imagination strongly applied to the study of reality
discovers that the borderline between the marvelous and the positive,
or, if you prefer, between the visible and the invisible universes,
is very faint..."

—Louis Pauwels and Jacques Bergier, *Le Matin des Magicians*

Imagination is more important than knowledge.
Knowledge is limited. Imagination encircles the world.

—Albert Einstein, *What I Believe*

But anyway, that brings us to what we're going to discuss here—
enjoying life and being special. Everyone is Special, you know.

—Benjamin Holt, *The Tao of Pooh*

♡ SYNOPSIS OF ♡
The Body Talks...and I Can Hear It

Magical Essence of Being in part continues a "story" that was begun in a previous volume, *The Body Talks...and I Can Hear It*. It also deepens and extends the information introduced in *The Body Talks*. The following brief summary of the first book introduces the reader to the characters in both books and catches the reader up to the point where the story picks up in this volume.

The Body Talks...and I Can Hear It begins with a **Being** in a beautiful meadow, pondering its Is-ness. The **Being** is trying to describe its Self (to its Self), but in so doing—no form is forthcoming. From out of the Eternal Moment of Now, first an awareness, then a voice, makes itself heard and knowable to this **Being.** The voice introduces itself as the **Being**'s "physical body representative" and describes its jurisdiction and duties as one of the **Being**'s "three foundational members for expression in third-dimensional reality." In short order, the **Being** finds itself able to "see" a symbolic representation of its physical body, in the form of a sleek, powerful **Jaguar**. With the **Jaguar**'s help, the **Being** likewise calls forth images to speak for its mental body (which appears in the form of a rather impatient, critical **Wizard**) and its emotional body (in the form of a timid **Deer**).

The **Being** realizes that because it is experiencing various pains, aches, and feelings of woe, perhaps it could use some help in clearing and balancing each of these three "dense-body" members. **Jaguar** suggests that they all attend the annual "Human Body Parts Symposium," where they might learn more about all three members' proper functions, as well as the ways that unresolved and unreleased mental and emotional issues and upsets get stored in the physical body. These stored upsets tend to prevent humans from flourishing in the ways that they would like to, and they also prevent humans from being "gotten," or fully understood and acknowledged, by others.

At the Symposium, all manner of physical human body parts are present, but the convention can barely be called to order, because so many of the body parts are filled to near-nonfunctioning with their agonies and stresses. The **Being** brings some of its own natural wisdom to bear, in this case leading the audience through a process that helps relieve all the body parts present of at least the most pressing of the major upsets that they are carrying. (*The Body Talks...*, pp. 44-52.)

To the grateful emcee (a **Foot**), the **Being** then expresses its burning question, concerning how and where upsets get stored in the physical body, and also how to gain balance between its members, so that it can understand and grasp their communications. At this point, **Astro**, a mysterious "Astral Body Therapist" steps forward, offering to cover exactly those topics, even though it means a change in the day's schedule. **Foot** graciously agrees, and **Astro** describes the typical interplay between a human being's emotional and mental members. It turns out that even though the mental and emotional bodies are designed to support each human Being and help it function through life, quite often they function at odds, with the mental member attempting to override the functions of the emotional and/or physical members—all in the name of "protecting" the **Being**, "coping" with life circumstances, or "keeping things under control." (See the imaginary discussion between "Harry" the emotional base and "Frank" the mental base, *The Body Talks*, pp. 57-59.) At the end of **Astro**'s story of Harry and Frank, **Deer** and **Wizard**, sitting among the audience, can only silently ponder their own unfortunate similarity to the two described by **Astro**.

Astro then goes on to humorously describe the exact issues and concerns that get stored in particular areas of the body, in both their mental and emotional locations and versions. With much boisterous interplay, the assembled body parts further express and validate their built-up frustrations and concerns about helping their respective human Beings to function and be received by other people. (pp. 61-114)

During a break in the Symposium, the **Being** rushes to catch up with **Astro** outside the symposium hall, determined to find out how it can apply all this theory and achieve some balance among its members as it goes about experiencing life. **Astro** seats the **Being** and its members under a shady tree and explains in depth the roles of the three foundational members. Then **Astro** illustrates how human Beings tend to be either *emotionally-based* or *mentally-based* in their languaging, which accounts for different ways of expressing themselves verbally and also for many miscues in communication between people. Also, when the three foundational members are out of balance, the difficulties become intensified, often to the point of complete communication breakdown, both within the person and in their "outer" relationships.

When **Astro** describes the mental nature's penchant for overriding the functions of the other members (in the name of "protecting" the Being), **Deer** bursts out its frustration at **Wizard** for doing "just that, all the time!" **Wizard** in turn, blazes sarcastically at **Deer** for being "such a wimp," and **Deer**, having finally had *enough*, explodes in pent-up rage.

While all this takes place, **Astro** quickly reassures the **Being** that only during the moment of upset does the emotional body actually gain the opportunity to grow, and that its cleansing function *must* be supported, even if it appears attack-oriented at first. Once cleared, the emotional member is more apt to speak for itself from within its own viewing place. Nonetheless, the **Being** feels increasingly hopeless about itself and humanity in general.

Astro then leads the **Being** through several processes to help its members cleanse, clear, and realign, including effective ways to:

(1) release old, negative programming (pp. 153-156)

(2) open up clear communications between the **Being** and its members (pp. 166-180), and

(3) straighten out the members' roles to support and fully express the **Being** while the **Being** is in human form (pp. 181-200) and in relationships to its Self and others.

During these processes, the **Being**'s imaginary vision of each of its members transforms into a new expression. Jaguar changes into a beautiful **Unicorn**, Wizard transforms into a sparkling **Amethyst Crystal**, and Deer emerges as a joyous, loving **Gabriella**, the spirit of the golden retriever dog that had once been the Being's constant companion and confidante for many earth years.

The book concludes with the group returning to the Human Body Parts Symposium, where all those present appear to have gone through a similar growth, clearing, and balancing process. Meanwhile, **Astro,** the Astral Body Therapist, slips away unnoticed, as mysteriously as it had appeared.

And now, in this volume, we encounter the newer expressions of the **Being**'s members—**Unicorn** (the Being's physical body representative), **Amethyst Crystal** (representing the mental body), and **Gabriella** (for the emotional body), along with the spiritual **Being,** almost one year after the Human Body Parts Symposium.

You have to find a way to consciously connect to the feeling
of "connection"—pure positive vibration, the Higher energy stream—
before you will recognize that you are deviating from it.

—"Abraham" through Esther Hicks

Tears cleanse the mind and the body and make us see the sense
of things. Life is chaos, you know.
It's only right that we cry now and then.
It brings things back into proper perspective.

—Catherine Coulter, *The Nightingale Legacy*

We should take care not to make the intellect our God;
it has, of course, powerful muscles, but no personality.

—Albert Einstein

We exist in our Minds...
We Live in our Hearts.

—Printed on the back of a *GLO* card

♡ MAGICAL ESSENCE OF BEING: ♡
HUMAN AND DIVINE

The Characters

The Being A spiritual consciousness known as a Human Being

Unicorn The Being's physical body representative

Amethyst Crystal The Being's mental body representative

Gabriella The Being's emotional body representative

Astro A mysterious teacher who refers to itself as an "Astral Body Therapist"

♡ PROLOGUE ♡

To begin our journey together, please get into a comfortable position, allowing your physical form to feel relaxed and taking three deep breaths, in through your nose and out through your mouth, emitting a soft sigh. As your breath takes on an easy rhythm, allow your eyes to close, and feel the ebb and flow of oxygen gently filling your lungs and dispersing throughout your physical form. Give yourself several minutes to enjoy the soothing benefits of watching your breath from within, allowing it to melt away all cares and concerns in this moment. Just like waves upon the sand, your breath follows the waves as they leisurely come onto the shore and then leisurely flow back out to sea....

And now, having your full yet relaxed attention, we ask you to envision your Self, your internal consciousness, in a beautiful forest. It is not so dense a forest that you cannot see the stars, for it is twilight, and the huge full moon shines its light among the redwood and pine trees, lighting up this peaceful forest. And as you wander through this natural wonderland, please notice the lushness of the vegetation and the friendliness of the forest animals as well as the soothing sounds of a stream as it easily makes its way toward a larger body of water. Perhaps some night birds are calling and the crickets are signaling to each other about your presence. After a while, you come upon a clearing in the forest, large enough to see quite a bit of the night sky. Here you let yourself find a soft matting of grass on which to rest your physical form.

Gazing up at the twinkling lights, just notice how marvelous the sky looks, as no city lights are near enough to dim the view. You can see the Milky

Way galaxy in its full magnificence as well as the better-known constellations and astrological star clusters.

Having familiarized yourself with the night sky and feeling quite at ease in the forest, we'd like you now to unzip your skin-suit and step out of it into a sense of freedom, breathing in the sparkling glow of star fire. Allow yourself as conscious awareness to release your Self completely from your physical form as well as from your thoughts and feelings. As you let your Self or Essence out, notice that the glow of star fire lights up your Essence just enough to see that you still have a *hint* of form, even though you are without physical form at this time. Notice also that "you" actually appear to be a little larger than your physical skin-suit, because your Essence is designed to puff out the skin-suit, to give it shape.

Now, in order to get acquainted with your Self as Essence or Awareness, please take what looks like an arm and easily reach up and touch the moon. Not hindered or limited by form, you most effortlessly extend your conscious awareness to reach the moon's surface, and you can really touch the moon, while the silver cord of continuity keeps you attached to your earthly experience as well.

Now, bring that extension of your Self back to the resemblance of your physical form, as you take what looks like the hint of a leg and let it extend way down into the Earth. Let your leg stretch past limestone caverns, crystal formations, and underground springs, until you know you've reached the core of the Earth. There, let your awareness gather all sensations and visual pictures, and see whether the core seems red hot or dark cold—or perhaps it seems endless as you view it from the inner depths of the Earth. Please remember there is no one form or one way to perceive this experience but rather only the expansion of you as Essence or Spirit or Conscious Awareness. In other words, despite anything suggested by the words given here, whatever you see, sense, or feel is perfect for you.

Once again, after a thorough observation, allow the thin silver cord of continuity to return you to the clearing in the forest as a glowing Essence, similar to but a little greater than your physical form. As you enjoy this state of Essence, or Being-ness, you gradually become aware that you are not alone in this lush green magical forest, for into the clearing under the sparkling night sky have also appeared the luminescent forms of an iridescent white **Unicorn** and a brilliant deep purple **Amethyst Crystal**....

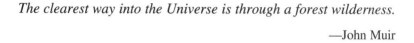

The clearest way into the Universe is through a forest wilderness.
—John Muir

There's no reality except the one contained within us.
—"Vanishing Son"

The World's a tiny piece of round,
And Magic Land is all around...
So open up your eye and ear,
And Magic Land will now appear.
—James S. Wallerstein, *Tommy & Julie*

♡ CHAPTER ONE ♡

A GIST OF WHAT'S AMISS

Amethyst Crystal: *(sounding agitated)* So who called this meeting, anyway?

Unicorn: *(responding sweetly yet thinking how irritable Amethyst Crystal, the mental body representative, has been lately)* You know I did.

*(Settling down in the lush forest greenery while waiting for Gabriella and the Being to arrive, Unicorn allows itself to more fully recall that same wonderful day almost a year ago when Astro, an Astral Body Therapist, magically appeared at the Annual Symposium of Human Body Parts. Unicorn begins to chuckle as it recalls the conversation of "Harry" and "Frank"—Astro's nicknames for the emotional nature that holds issues in the **left** side of the body, and the mental nature that stores items in the **right** side of the body—and how "Harry" and "Frank" typically relate.[1])*

(Meanwhile, Gabriella, the emotional body representative, enters the forest clearing unnoticed by either Unicorn or Amethyst Crystal.)

---

[1] See *The Body Talks...and I Can Hear It*, pp. 57-59.

Gabriella: *(startling Unicorn out of its reverie)* That was quite a story, wasn't it?

Unicorn: *(a bit unnerved)* Must you sneak into the moment so silently? Just because we both live in the moment doesn't mean I always want you present.

Gabriella: *(raising an eyebrow)* I didn't realize that either one of us *owned* the moment.

Unicorn: *(with a sigh)* You're right, of course. I'm just a little edgy these days—and not sleeping well, either. That's why I finally called this gathering.

Gabriella: *(admitting its own frustration)* I was aware of your discomfort but unable to soothe you, what with Amethyst Crystal's constant mutterings.

Unicorn: *(with a lop-sided smile)* I admit that lately I've even thought about giving our mental member a muzzle, at least at night so I can sleep—knowing full well that I am no more in charge of it than it is of me.

Gabriella: I can't say that I blame you; our mental counterpart used to *always* think it had jurisdiction over me *and* our Being's feelings—so I suppose, in a pinch, it too might try to revert to its old habits, when upset. By the way, where is our Being, at the moment?

Unicorn: *(a little surprised)* I'm wondering that myself. *(now with true concern)* You don't suppose anything has happened to her?

Gabriella: *(thinking out loud)* I don't feel so, but something is amiss—I can feel it.

(At that moment, the Being stumbles into the magical forest clearing, obviously exhausted and looking more than a little piqued.)

Amethyst Crystal: *(even more agitated than before)* So there you are! We have been waiting for you. What in the world took you so long? *(even though it has been but a moment since the get-together was announced)*

The Being: *(put out by this reception)* Hey, what ever happened to "Hi— it's great to see you again!" *(The Being looks pointedly at Amethyst Crystal.)*

Gabriella: *(hoping to defuse the tension in the air)* Never mind that now—we're all here, and that's what matters.

(As the Being looks around at its three densest means of self-expression, its internal awareness lights on Unicorn, its representative in the physical realm, noticing that somehow the Unicorn does not appear quite as vibrant as usual. And then its awareness takes in Gabriella, its emotional member, always available with a kind word of encouragement. At last—and very much not the least—its gaze comes to rest on Amethyst Crystal, its mental means of expressing in the third dimension, who is sparkling its deep purple brilliance in a proud and defiant manner.)

Being: *(its exhaustion momentarily drowned out by a bubbling over of appreciation)* So, here we are. Can you all believe that it's been almost one year since we began consciously working together—and just look at all our changes. For starters, you, Unicorn, look like you've lost some weight. And Gabriella— I do believe the twinkle is back in your eye. And not to be left out, Amethyst Crystal, your deep purple facets are all aglow—and I know I'm more healthy, happy, and organized than ever before—even though I'm a bit tired today.

Amethyst Crystal: *(impatiently pressing its question)* Fine, fine, fine. That's all well and good. But what about *eternity*?

(All conversation stops abruptly, and Amethyst Crystal takes advantage of having all of their collective attention.)

Amethyst Crystal: This living moment-to-moment is all well and good, but what about *me*? I want to grow, too. Sure, it's great that we have our life more in order, and of course every human Being wants physical health—and I'd be an ogre to even hint that you as a Being would want to be anything but happy— but I repeat myself: *What about me?*

(starting to raise its voice and picking up speed) It's not just that I've "in the past" considered myself the driving force for our mutual unfoldment or that I need to have my energy field patted all the time with a few words like *Good job* or *Great support.* I'm asking, ***What about me?***—the one member who is in charge of past-future, or All of Eternity—for, whether I go forward or backward, I always return to the same place!

(Amethyst Crystal looks around, finds all mouths gaping questioningly, and continues to voice its upset with escalating intensity.) Call it "in the beginning"—of which there is no beginning—or "far out to distant galaxies and beyond"—of which there is no time or end to the universe—I'm asking, ***WHAT ABOUT ME?!?!***

(Unicorn, Gabriella, and the Being are all glued to their spots, dumbfounded by the breadth of the question that has obviously weighed heavily on Amethyst Crystal's mind for a

long while, causing it a great deal of consternation, and which, at the moment, truly poses a dilemma to each of them.)

(The silence continues as each only begins to grasp the enormity of the question.)

Amethyst Crystal: Well, that certainly got all your attention. Now, can you begin to see what has been eating away at me? I'm happy to help you all, and I really do feel that a team has been created, and I can even see the results in our Being's life as we work together to achieve a particular goal. But haven't you noticed just how *repetitious* all this is? I mean, how many times can you enthusiastically make the bed *again* or feed yourself *again* or go work out *again*?

Don't you see, it's not enough for me just to assist all of you. I have to explore the part of us known as the Greater Self, or our Divinity, or Universal Self, or Oneness. And now that my energy is not just focused on surviving in human terms, I ought to be freed up to expand my range of interests and share that realm with all of you here while we are on planet Earth among humans and other life forms. I mean, doesn't that make sense?

Gabriella: *(taking advantage while Amethyst Crystal takes a breath)* Are you implying that we have been holding you back? Like it's our fault or something?

Amethyst Crystal: *(defensively)* Now there you go. And you used to accuse *me* of putting notions onto *you*. Can't you see, I just have to grow, in Earth terms—like you have, and if I do, maybe you would then discover that something comes out of it even for you, on a grander scale!

Unicorn: *(still confused by Amethyst Crystal's upset)* Excuse me for my ignorance, but are you saying that you think the past and future are one, but you're not sure?

Amethyst Crystal: *(determined to express itself precisely)* What I'm saying is, *like you, I must explore and grow and expand*—and that means something entirely different for me than for you, at least when it comes to the way I go about it. I'm only saying, *I don't know, but I must proceed!*

(A deep silence fills the air, after which the Being finally ventures an inquiry.)

The Being: *(tentatively)* You sound frustrated, Amethyst Crystal. Are you?

Amethyst Crystal: *(replying in a huff)* Well, wouldn't you be? After all, I'm one of the means for you to Self-express. Haven't you noticed lately just how *repetitious* your life on planet Earth has seemed—as in, exactly how many times can you go shopping, get gas for the car, pay bills, make phone calls, get your nails done, go to work, run errands, shower, eat. I mean, *you* don't even have a husband and children to care for, and *still* your activities are done over and over and over again! *Highly* repetitious, don't you think?

The Being: *(a bit dumbfounded)* Well, I guess I've been so focused on getting my Earth life in order that I truly hadn't noticed. Now that you mention it, though, as soon as I get into a really great routine, I tend to drop something out, just to vary things. I thought I was just being lazy—but maybe there is more to it than that.

Gabriella: *(breaking in)* Now that you mention it, Being, I've seen that kind of lapse in myself as well. For example, I've noticed myself entering relationships so enthused and excited and ready to take on the world—only to find myself lulled into a stupor at some point. And then I end up thinking less of the other person or less of myself. Is that what you are talking about, Amethyst Crystal?

Amethyst Crystal: *(clearly, but still distressed)* I can't speak for you, of course, as our various means of contributing to this life are different, but even still, what you mention could be related. My frustration is that I don't know exactly *what* I'm looking for or how to proceed. *(almost screaming now) Where is that Astral Body Therapist, when we really need some help??!*

(Unicorn, Gabriella, and the Being all sit quietly, pondering the uneasiness that Amethyst Crystal has stirred up in each of them. Then, Amethyst Crystal, tired from voicing its frustrations—and Unicorn and Gabriella, both filled with a depth of uncertainty—all turn toward the Being, seeking some clarity, only to see the Being filled with a vague sense of something missing in life.)

(As each takes in the other, knowing that no answer is forthcoming at this instant, they collectively get up and move to separate areas within the clearing to ponder the situation. Within minutes, quiet rhythmic breathing indicates that all have fallen asleep, partly from exhaustion and partly from the uncertainty caused by this quandary.)

It's past time to merely survive...it's time to really thrive!

—Gail Coffey

If I am 'out of tune' with my Self, all of my perceptual views
of the outer world become distorted.
Transformation comes when my sense of Self
is greater than my perceptions.

—Rev. Matthew McNaught

Crises are a challenge to move into something new;
a challenge to adapt. ...
Each stage of evolution becomes the platform for the next stage.

—*The Global Brain*

CHAPTER TWO

A MYSTICAL MAGICAL DREAM REALITY

(The three dense body members and the Being each move into the dream state and unbeknown to each other begin to recall Astro and how that cosmic traveler assisted them almost a year ago at the Annual Symposium of Human Body Parts. For Astro had helped them clear themselves as to their respective areas of jurisdiction, so each could do a better job and work more fully with the other members, in assisting their Being in extending the quality of her Self-expression in third-dimensional reality.)

(Then, as if the mere thought of Astro had willed its presence to appear in their individual dreams, Astro's vibratory field enters the clearing in the magical forest and begins to converse with each of them simultaneously, engaging all their awarenesses in one concurrent process.)

Astro: *(appearing to each of the members and the Being separately and simultaneously)* As you sleep here in this forest clearing, I would have you take a journey, a greater adventure than you have yet to conceive. To do so—and I might remind you that you are already freed from the constraints of a human skin-suit—you must let go of your "Self" as any "form" to which you are used to considering yourself. Please take a moment to do this….

(Astro pauses both for effect and for each member and the Being to relax into the dream state.)

Now we will experientially grow into a greater awareness of Self—and once there we will envision the nature of our united knowingness. To do this, I ask you now to use your breath to enhance your ability to expand. So, while taking deep full breaths, I'd like you to see your Self as having grown so huge that you can easily place your hint of a right arm into the Atlantic Ocean—and your hint of a left arm into the Pacific, while you give the entire continental United States a big warm hug. Feel the pulsating vibrating energy that you are as you extend yourself out from the heart of your being to each and every one of the forty-eight states and the life force that makes up the continental portion of America....

Now, taking another deep breath, allow your Self to expand even further—entirely outside the Earth's atmosphere—and simply and easily wrap what appears to have the vague energy resemblance of arms and legs entirely around the Earth, giving the whole planet a huge energy-packed hug. Feel that your intention and vibrating life force spark a planetary glow as the Earth receives your heart-felt joy and appreciation for being your home.

Once you can see the planet respond to your personal contribution, I'd like you to take another lung-and-belly-filled breath as we now lose sight of you as a hint of form. Not having any particular avenue of expression at this point, you now begin to feel your Self as the space in which your entire solar system exists.

(Astro merges with the Being and each of its members to feel their shift in awareness.)

Notice that all of the planets, the stars, the many moons, and the Sun are all contained within you as the space in which they naturally orbit the Sun. At this time, I want you to look and see just how large planet Earth appears to you in reference to the other planets and stars within you. Also from this space let your Self look around and see if there is any trace of fear or worry within your awareness, or if by chance it feels amazingly calm while the solar system goes about its business. You might even want to take a moment, just for curiosity's sake, to check and see whether any planet is even slightly out of its orbit or if any star seems out of place....

Just note the experience, whatever it may be, for you, as you. You might want to spend some time here, enjoying the natural perfection of it all, or however the status appears, allowing your conscious awareness to relax and merge with the tranquility. However, I must inform you that we have further to go....

(Astro relaxes its Self in the process, as the feeling of Spaceness envelops it.)

So when you are ready, simply continue to breathe and allow yourself to expand out even further. I now want you to imagine your Self as the vastness in which the entire Milky Way exists. Yes, that may include many thousands of solar systems, each with their own sun, planets, and star systems. Just bask in the brightness of so much sparkle and light, in perfect orchestration, in the vastness that you are, noticing that planet Earth is no longer the focus of your viewing place. In fact, it is no longer visible, except as a teeny tiny speck of awareness, in a teeny tiny solar system....

(Astro, after pausing once again to take in the wonder of it all, continues speaking.)

Astro: And now, from this peaceful, floaty openness, I ask you to take one final, full-blown breath, to release any notion of spaciousness and to expand yourself out now so far as to include the *entire Universe*. That means *all* of the galaxies, including the Milky Way, *all* of the suns in the many solar systems, and *all* of the stars whose light doesn't even reach our own night's sky. I mean, feel your Self lose all sense of dimension, with total freedom of time, space, and distance— and just *be* the wholeness in which everything exists as Totality. Give your Self or spirit permission to release any limitation, any judgment, any description, and enjoy the Being-ness of eternity, the exquisite balance and harmony that just *is* and *isn't* all at the same time, from the human vantage point, feeling that no one and no thing is left out of this wondrous sensation of pure momentary bliss....

(Astro pauses for a good while to allow each of the dreamers to expand and fully experience this omnipresent awareness, and it merges with the Oneness as well.)

(Several Eternal Moments of Now pass by before Astro gently enters the dream state awareness of the Being, Unicorn, Amethyst Crystal, and Gabriella once again.)

(Within the wholeness, the dreamers hear Astro's familiar voice as if it were their own.)

Astro: In the beginning is the **Eternal Moment of Now**—whole and all-inclusive, timeless and undefined.... And after eons of this **Now-ness,** this Totality moves into a consciousness of wanting to know its Self, with no idea of how that might come to pass. So over more endless timeless-ness, this awareness becomes so strong that it begins to vibrate into a *sound,* such as **Om,** for example, and at the same moment of now, it emerges as radiant white **Light.** And over more and more periods of *no-time, no-form* eventually provides enough *oomph* to create form, or *is-ness* and *isn't-ness*—or as those in the Far East say, the original dichotomy, *yin* and *yang*—or as we in the West might say, the dichotomy of **nature** and **magic,** which represents all of eternity or reality as we know it. This awareness of being conscious of everything in perfect harmony and balance is known to us as Love, and gradually this Love becomes the space in which, say, six viewing spaces or perceptual places evolve that equally represent the whole. And from there, formlessness begins to emerge truly as form and eventually organizes itself into human expression, while remaining linked to Totality. And, from your position as a witness, you observe that as each human emerges into form, it does so from one of those six vantage points or viewing spaces. I want to suggest that those six invisible perceptual holographic viewing places could be called, for want of a better description, "**Magical Essences**"—even though the consciousness of each view is invisible and indescribable.

(Once again, Astro pauses as it feels the fullness of Cosmic Connection.)

Astro: If you could capture each view in words, you might imagine a gist of a special quality to each of the six Essences or perceptual awarenesses. Please allow me to suggest some names to embody those special qualities as we take a tour around the spokes of this gigantic, universal wheel of cosmic perception. The first quality we encounter is the *Angelic* quality of *Connectedness.* And floating opposite this viewing place we experience the **Wizard** dynamic of *Intensity*. Continuing to float along into another view of your total Self, you intuit an exhilarating **Fairy** vibration of *Lightness,* and opposite this lightness you locate a **Dwarvian** vibration of *Groundedness.* Finally, your awareness is captured by an **Elvian** characteristic of *Mischievous Motion,* before it lightly touches down upon the **Unicorn** essence of *Profound Belief.*

(Astro's voice soothingly continues to lead the Being and its members—and unknowingly, its Self as well—through this lullaby of dreamland. As Astro continues its soliloquy, it is no longer aware if the Being and its members are even half-hearing its melodic thought-flow in their collective dream.)

Astro: And then, still from your vantage point as an observer to a magnificent process unfolding, imagine that as every human Being funnels from Totality into form through one of these perceptual doorways or viewing places, each individual emerges and speaks its Self through one of two very different bases of communication—from either the avenue of emotional truth, which can be called the **emotional base,** or the language of thoughts and visions, that is, the **mental base.**

(In this moment of now, all the dreamers merge with the dream, including the energy known as Astro, as all of Totality and all of Humanity, weaving the webs of eternity and infinity into a moment of Bliss.)

(Finally, Astro, returning from forever and now, sighs contentedly before continuing.)

Astro: And now, having clearly experienced this holographic awareness of wholeness as permeating every atom and molecule that make up the universe and each individual human

Being in that universe—we begin the journey back to your human awareness.

So, without losing your sense of Oneness—feel your Self return to the vastness that is the galaxy known as the Milky Way, and you find you are drawn as if by a magnet toward one of these six magical doorways to wholeness. A sense of shrinking sometimes enters awareness at this point—and sometimes not—as the Milky Way galaxy is huge in its own right.

And with a conscious effort, condense your Self now a bit further, so that you might feel your Self as the space of your solar system, without forgetting that you are also One with All. Take time to notice that the Earth is not the largest planet in this particular solar system....

At this point, with another cosmic breath, you are able to condense your Self even further, as you even more succinctly identify with one of the Magical Essences or perceptual viewing places as you head toward human form. Eventually, you emerge into the merest hint of form, which enables you to wrap your energy once again around the entire planet Earth— this time with an even greater sense of unconditional Love. Then, as you reenter the Earth's atmosphere, notice that your human awareness has gotten stronger, and also your sense of Magical Essence, as you give your home continent an even stronger hug, for you have the knowledge and the experience of Totality within you, as invisible pure magic within the hint of form....

(Astro continues to guide the dreamers from the invisible toward the visible realms.)

Astro: And lastly, I ask you bring your wholeness to its most condensed and defined form, known as a human Being, with a physical, a mental, and an emotional body representative. All the while, remember that you are or live in a porous body that expresses Totality in *visible* nature and that allows your Being-ness to be eternally linked in Light and Love with the All, through your chosen viewing place—be it **Angelic, Fairy, Elvian, Unicorn, Dwarvian,** or **Wizard.**

(Astro pauses a moment for the dreamers to complete their arrival as Magical Essence in human form.)

Then, when you feel rested enough, allow your Self to reclaim your sense of Self, in whatever form you are most familiar with—be it as spiritual Being, visionary mental function, emotional feelings, or physical body. Notice that you have returned to your "form" as you know it in third-dimensional terms, fully rested and refreshed, here in the magical forest.

(Astro falls silent and slips out of the collective dream, as the four dreamers now begin to stir and awaken.)

> *I am the weaver,*
> *I am the woven one.*
> *I am the Dreamer*
> *I am the Dream.*
> —Native American song

Don't ever be afraid to dream,
Because dreams are what we are.

—from a song by Charles Kennedy

One feels as if one has been dissolved and merged into nature.

—Albert Einstein

...they'd been the Oneness, floating like the wind,
dancing with the pulse of the Universe, singing and chanting
in harmony with the beat of the Creator. In that manner,
they'd felt the twirling beauty of the spinning stars,
heard the songs of distant suns, and felt the pulse of life ... the memory
clung ... with the rich sweetness of warm honey.

—W. Michael Gear and Kathleen O'Neal Gear, *People of the Fire*

Merging with Totality

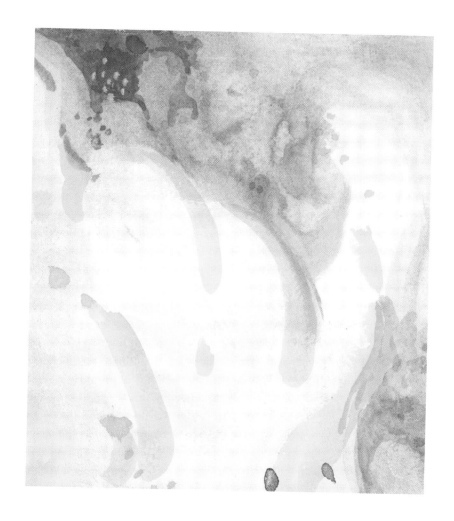

The

Angelic

Essence

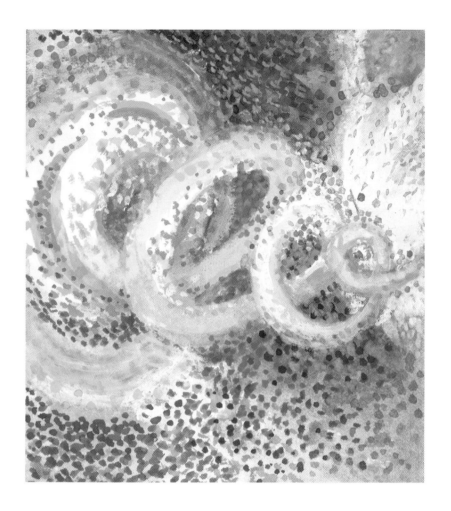

The

Fairy

Essence

The

Elvian

Essence

The

Unicorn

Essence

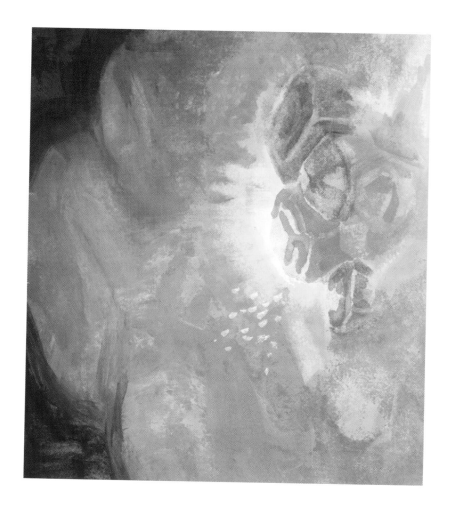

The

Dwarvian

Essence

The

Wizard

Essence

Re-Emerging Into Form

A UNIVERSAL WAKE-UP CALL

(Amethyst Crystal, Unicorn, Gabriella, and the Being slowly come out of their individual dreams and into awareness of themselves, and, each in their own time, open their eyes. However, they do not notice the presence of Astro nearby.)

Amethyst Crystal: *("awake" now, looking around at the others and, being mental, quick to express)* What a wonderful dream I had! Astro was there—and in living color, too!

(Before Amethyst Crystal can continue, both Unicorn and Gabriella, talking over each other, pipe in.)

Gabriella and Unicorn: Me, too!… Astro was in my dream, too!… What fun!… I feel so refreshed!

The Being: *(trying to get a word in edgewise)* Whoa! It seems we all had a lovely, similar experience.

Astro: *(without any forewarning of its presence)* Not similar— identical!

(Unicorn squeals in surprise, while Gabriella and Amethyst Crystal practically jump out of the skins they were not in— and the Being darts clean out of the clearing—at the sound of Astro's voice behind them.)

Astro: *(with a grin)* Gotcha!

The Being: *(returning to the forest and the first to regain its voice)* You sure did—and took pleasure in it, I see!

(At the Being's attempt to make a point, Astro, a good-natured cosmic traveler, laughs even louder.)

(Finally gathering their wits about them and really glad to see Astro, the Being and its three members converge on Astro, almost suffocating it with affection, hugs, and hellos.)

Astro: And I'm glad to see you, as well.

(All talking at once, the three members and the Being launch in with their questions.)

All: What happened last year? Where did you go? We thought we would never see you again! Who are you, anyway?

Astro: *(continuing to take pleasure from the reunion and still not answering any of the questions)* I see you all haven't lost your knack for questions. . . . I believe you were just asking for me?

Gabriella and Unicorn: *(talking right over Amethyst Crystal)* Oh, yes! Poor Amethyst Crystal is fit to be tied—not with any of us, but with the Universe or Eternity, or some such thing—and we were lost and didn't know how to proceed . . . and thought of you, and . . .

Astro: Whoa, there! *(noting with precise accuracy)* Now *this* energy *does* feel familiar. . . . One question at a time, please.

Amethyst Crystal: *(jumping in before the others can speak)* I have just got to know, Astro—where were we just now?—in the dream, I mean. And how is it that we all had the same dream, with you in it?

Astro: *(barely concealing a smile)* To tell you the truth, we were accessing All Knowledge or Knowing-ness—through the thin veil of dreaming, which is another means of accessing the Self—and actually a holographic extension of *you,* Amethyst Crystal, as the mental body. That is, we were in **dreamtime awareness,** courtesy of the dream dimension that links up with a human Being's mental member, just on a grander scale.

Amethyst Crystal: *(dumbfounded)* What?! *Expanded dimension of myself?*

Astro: That's right—and there's much more to each of you than we discussed at last year's Symposium. In fact, each of you has three known levels, each of these with different approaches to the same question—whatever the question is!

Amethyst Crystal: *(sensing the glimmer of an answer to its dilemma)* But why didn't you mention any of this before?

Astro: *(chuckling at the cosmic humor)* Well, you did ask just now, didn't you? As the saying goes, when the question gets asked, the Universe responds, or when the student is ready, the teaching appears. It is obviously time to expand your horizons—at least as far as nine known vibrational levels that humans express themselves through—call them *holographic links* or *expanded bodies* if you like—while in form on planet Earth. Even then, I say *nine* only because who knows how many there are, in reality. You do recall me referring to all of you—Amethyst Crystal, Unicorn, and Gabriella—as the *three denser members*—right?

Amethyst Crystal: *(getting nervous)* You mean we may have to add in six more members and still come from individual expression in our own arenas as well as interlink with each other?

Astro: *(chuckling out loud)* Sounds next to impossible, doesn't it?

Gabriella: *(a bit uneasy and on the verge of feeling overwhelmed)* Sure, but will we have to meet these energies in person?

Unicorn: *(almost interrupting and slightly horrified)* Even invite them to our gatherings?!?

(The three dense-body representatives feel a bit proprietary of their new-found connectedness and are also worried about uncontrolled pandemonium at future official board meetings.)

Astro: My, my, my—but are we once again up to that unknown called *change*? After all, it certainly seems that just when a body gets settled into its Self as a means of expressing the Being, all of a sudden there's more to deal with?

(At this, Amethyst Crystal, Unicorn, and Gabriella all look a little sheepish for being more concerned about their individual positions than about the opportunity for growth for their Being.)

Astro: Actually... *(Astro pauses for effect—and to be sure that all three members and the Being are listening)*, these so-called *other bodies* are not separate from you at all, but rather larger awarenesses or levels of unfoldment of each of you.

(The Being, Gabriella, Unicorn, and Amethyst Crystal, looking totally confused, send their combined consciousness directly at Astro, nearly knocking the cosmic traveler off its perch.)

Astro: *(regaining its composure)* Let me explain it another way. Perhaps we can refer to the nine "bodies" in terms of a **Lower, Middle,** and **Higher Self**—the Lower level referring to density, like yourselves, with Middle connections through each of you that link to the greater awareness, or Higher Self functions. In other words, each of you—Unicorn as the physical body representative, Amethyst Crystal as the mental body representative, and even you, Gabriella, as the emotional body representative—have universal connections on at least these two other levels.

*(As Astro stops to gather its thoughts, the Being begins to feel a sense of breakthrough to that **something** it has been missing or seeking for a very long time.)*

Astro: *(continuing uninterrupted)* More specifically, you, Unicorn, the densest or **Physical** member, expand into the "Middle realm" as the **Subtle Physical Body,** where the chakras and the aura exist. You might call the aura an electromagnetic field, and the major chakras a set of at least seven known energy-sensitive centers, or swirling energy vortexes, located along the physical spine from the tailbone area to the top of the head or beyond. For who knows how many chakras there are, really. *(Astro sends its rhetorical cosmic question in Unicorn's direction before continuing.)*

From there, Unicorn, your holographic form leaps to a larger awareness, call it the **Witness Self** or **Soul,** as your invisible and unlimited human link to Totality. In the dream we just shared, the Witness Self enabled you to "watch" as well as participate in the dream at the same time. All of these levels are You—but for simplicity let's call them your Lower, Middle, and Upper Self, and all are means of expression for that particular spirit of oneness known as your Being, with whom you interact and to whom you give form.

(As Astro begins to focus on Amethyst Crystal, Unicorn tunes out for the moment and turns inward to start filtering all that Astro has so casually shared about its many functions.)

Astro: *(enthralled with its own conversation)* As for you, Amethyst Crystal, the **Mental** body expands into an arena known as the **Ego**-centricity, which often takes a bad beating in Earth terms. You see, in your function as an Ego body, which corresponds to the Middle realm we are talking about, you are here to see that your Being stays most interested in advancing its Self. If this Ego function did not exist, the Being could easily wander off in consciousness as a tree, or a rubber hose, or the wind—and we would have a heck of a time figuring out what is what on planet Earth.

Then, on an even Higher realm of awareness, you function as the **Dream Awareness**—the level that enabled us to journey to a fantastic place of imagination just a few moments ago. All humans know that at some point during their sleep, they dream—whether they remember those dreams or not. And, as you so recently experienced, at this expanded level of consciousness, or *created thought,* all things are possible. Another way of expressing this Dream-realm of possibility is, *If you can dream it up, it is possible to be produced in form.*

(Astro now speaks directly to Amethyst Crystal.)

Astro: **It is at this higher level of consciousness that freedom from drudgery and repetition exists—of expanding into new horizons.** For example, today, we were "lucid dreaming," as each of you was aware of your Self in the dream.

(A lightning-quick shimmer of recognition passes through Amethyst Crystal, like an electric shock, at Astro's nailing exactly what had been ailing it, though it had not known how to express it.)

Astro: *(before Amethyst Crystal can pipe in with a comment)* And not to be forgotten or left out in importance, is you,

Gabriella—occupying the Being's **Emotional** connected-ness in its densest third-dimensional concerns. You expand on the Middle level to operate as the **Psychic-Intuitive Body,** where Wisdom is a given and miracles an every-moment possibility.

And, in a Higher, even more pervasive space, you operate as the **Vital Force,** or *Prana Shakti,* or *Chi* that is said to be at the basis of all things—**Pure Love,** expressed as vibration and energy. It has been said that if the Universe were to be destroyed tomorrow, then this *Prana* or *Chi* is so potent, conscious, and self-aware that it could create a whole new Universe.[1] This pure, expansive, vibrational energy has been known and harnessed in Earth's Far East for at least 1,000 years as *t'ai chi*—or "all of Reality"—and in India for many millennia through the yogic methods of developing self-awareness.

All these "bodies" or levels of consciousness are extended or vaster ways in which the eternal Self perceives and expresses its Self.

(Unicorn, Amethyst Crystal, and Gabriella, each absorbed in their own thoughts of just how incredibly awesome this thing called Life really is, look over to the Being with more respect than ever for the intricate balance of invisible and visible constituents that it is made up of.)

(Meanwhile, the Being, having sat quietly while listening to Astro focus on its members, wonders a series of questions to its Self: "How is it that we have not been consciously aware of all these levels of functioning?... And if we are so cosmi-

---

[1] See Sri Aurobindo, *On Prana,* and Dr. Hwang Wen-Shan (in reference to *Chi*), *Fundamentals of T'ai Chi Ch'uan.*

cally connected, then why do things get so mucked up at times?... And how can we possibly begin to imagine what it would take to clear our connection between all these bodies, so that we can be even more aware of who we are, as spirit-in-form—let alone relate to others equally endowed?")

Astro: *(once again impressed with the level of awareness in this Being and its members, replies to these unasked questions)* It's true, Being, that the natural connection to the cosmos for many humans is clouded over by the upsets they carry in their dense body systems: anger, rage, resentment, fear, hurt, bitterness, sadness, low self-esteem, lack of confidence, feelings of being less than full-value, lack of vitality and energy, and so on. Or, as adults, they've lost the connection with the purer or more connected state of their child-self, who is still feeling abandoned, attacked, belittled, discounted, run-over, frightened, or generally unsafe in life, even though the Being, in Earth-chronological terms, has reached a so-called "mature" physical body form.

The Being: *(jarred from within its Self at the realization that Astro was somehow **inside** it, and blurting out its first thought)* How did you do that!?!?

    (Astro, knowing exactly what the Being is referring to, simply smiles and continues with the lesson at hand.)

Astro: As you know from our previous experiences together, these dense-level upsets and blockages can be cleared using processes like those we engaged in during last year's Body Parts Symposium.[2] However, the connecting points from you three

---

[2] For some of these processes, see *The Body Talks...and I Can Hear It* (e.g., *Amphitheater Process*, p. 44; the *Internal Video Library*, p. 153; and the *Board Room (Changing Room) Process* (pp. 166, 181).

to your expanded or cosmic levels were not fully covered at last year's conference, largely because experience has shown us that a Being in upset literally has no "listen-ability" to change or growth. And so, as needed, we focused instead on first-things-first, that is, clearing and cleansing the Physical, Mental, and Emotional levels of expression.

(Astro gently enfolds the Being in nurturing awareness, to remind it that "upset" and "survival-mode" are not bad, just all-consuming whenever present.)

(Astro, pausing a moment, looks around and sees four silent and hopeful faces, now most eager to hear more about how to reach and work with the expanded or cosmic levels of themselves.)

Astro: *(proceeding to expound on the access to the Middle and Upper levels of the Self)* Interestingly enough, to open the connection between all the levels of the body systems, finding a way to clear and connect to the Middle level is the key. You see, the Middle realms are in close proximity to both *survival* (the Lower self) and *bliss* (the Higher self), and by addressing these Middle levels—such as working with the Subtle Physical Body and its energy patterns—the clearing can release buildup in both directions.

As hard as it is to believe, when one "awareness level" or "body" is down, all the other known means of Self-expression are affected. It's like having the idea to redecorate your house. That might be a fine idea, but if your basement is flooded and your foundation full of termites, chances are you won't be ready to focus on redoing the upstairs bathroom just yet.

However, if one level can purify itself (*i.e.,* get rid of the termites and dry out the basement), it uplifts the vibration of the other known means of communicating the Self. This in turn is why people like psychic readings and past-life regressions. They may even like dream interpretation and doing *t'ai chi* or *yoga,* or meditating on "God"—or Universe—if the Middle realms are sufficiently open to conscious input.

Again, by working from the Middle level of unfoldment, it is possible to clear out distortion in both directions to reach all the levels of Self-expression—by the very fact that the Middle bodies have a direct link to you, the densest systems, as well as to the higher, most expanded systems. Quite often, when this Middle level is cleared, a miracle seems to take place, because all levels (Lower, Middle, and Higher Self) get linked.

Through this type of clearing process, which is very personal and unique for each Being, a human Being can gain a more conscious connection to its most expanded levels of functioning. In other words, the Being **Re-Members** its Self. This frees it to explore the creative process through all its means of expression, including Dreaming, moving the Vital Force, being the Observer as well as the participant in its own life, developing its Intuition, and so on, as well as enjoying earthly pursuits such as home, family, work, and daily life.

(The Being, in quiet excitement, begins to catch a glimpse of the possibilities that such a conscious linking to all avenues of expression can hold for human Beings.)

Astro: *(looking over at the awed Being as it continues . . .)* That's right, Being, a full shift *can* take place in how a human Being holds its Self and the world it lives in.

(The Being, again surprised at Astro's answering its unspoken thoughts, is at a loss for words.)

Astro: *(continuing immediately)* At the same time, however, if these Middle realms are not accessible to a Being, and that Being operates strictly through its three denser members alone, then connection to the Higher Self is for all intents and purposes unattainable. And this only seems to further block the flow of Life, for **it's only in the full connection of all levels that the experiences of abundant flow and "miracles" become commonplace in daily living.**

Gabriella: *(full of excitement and practically shouting)* So, do we get to do more processes to clear these areas, like we did at last year's Symposium? *Do we, huh?*

(Astro, considering this question, pauses for a considerable length of time, then finally speaks.)

Astro: What you need to know, Gabriella, is that unlike the clearing processes for you denser systems, which speak directly to humanity's struggles to survive, these expanded realms are not so cut and dried. What I mean to say, is, at this level of awareness, the experience of the holographic or multi-dimensional Self is awakened, and each person literally has their own unique expression and understanding of the impact of this knowingness. It's like entering into a whole world through each individual's internal eyes. Such a process requires lots of both *time* and *timeless-ness,* in order to explore fully. However, it seems to me that today you have *already* opened the doorway into your own Higher realms—through the *Totality* process we have already shared—and at this point all systems are in fact accessed, and I would venture to say that you appear ready to proceed into even further explorations of your invisible aspects. Now, am I right?

(In union, Gabriella, Amethyst Crystal, and Unicorn vibrate their enthusiasm to continue to explore whatever it might be

that Astro intends to share next, while the Being, still in awe at Astro's ability to grasp their internal knowingness, silently gives a nod.)

(Astro continues to pause as it sees a light dawn in the Being's awareness.)

The Being: *(finally understanding that Astro receives direct thought patterns, says without words)* **Does this mean I can go "Home" in consciousness soon?**

(Astro, receiving the Being's thought, once again smiles lovingly.)

Life is large, bigger than the both of us,
Life is large, all you need is just a little trust.
—Pete and Maura Kennedy, from their song, "Life Is Large"

During your magical dawn, you were given the keys that would open, one after another, the mysterious passages of life, and of your life.
—Enrique Castillo Rincón

How can you get very far,
If you don't know Who You Are?
How can you do What You Ought,
If you don't know What You've Got.
—Winnie-the-Pooh, as quoted by Benjamin Holt in *The Tao of Pooh*

CHAPTER FOUR

RE-MEMBERING WHOLENESS

(The Being, Gabriella, Unicorn, and Amethyst Crystal, eager to hear more about their expanded and invisible aspects, muse on the implications of what Astro has already shared. Astro, meanwhile, remains silent to give the information a chance to ground itself within each of the listeners.)

Amethyst Crystal: *(usually quick to grasp, yet still fumbling to understand)* So, Astro, *exactly* how does knowing about our expanded levels help with daily living?

Astro: *(with a chuckle)* Well, for one thing, now you can begin to see why you all have been having so much difficulty representing your Being on planet Earth. When you are, in your densest forms, out of synch with each other, the human Being that you are here to serve has to get by in mere *survival mode.* And in survival mode, just getting through the day can be a major ordeal. For some, *survival* becomes simply getting enough food to eat or a place to sleep each and every day, and this endeavor occupies all their time and available energy. For others, *survival* may be how to avoid being abused again— whether the abuse is physical, mental, emotional, or a combination thereof. And for others, it may mean dealing with a physical, mental, or emotional handicap that they were either born with or developed along the way in life. Whenever a human Being has been operating on this *survival* level, if you were to speak of our "cosmic connection," quite likely that Being would not have a strong listen-ability to what you were talking about.

Amethyst Crystal: *(with a light dawning)* Oh, so that's what you meant, Astro, when you used the metaphor about the house whose foundation is full of termites, so the redecorating-of-the-upstairs-bathroom project gets put on hold. That's *survival?*

Astro: *Bingo!* And, as you begin to unfold the Middle realms for yourselves, you begin to discover that the **Ego** body's prime purpose is to see that *you* take care of *your Self.* Truly, no one else is signed up to "do" your life—every minute that you are in form—except you. And, if you aren't *on-line* (that is, *connected* or *Re-Membered)* with your Self, it is very difficult to be continually "up and supportive" of your Self, first, which then opens the possibility to be so for others.

When *way-off-line*, as it were, it is likewise difficult *not* to move into reaction, attack, blame, shame, guilt, and so on. Like a domino effect, during these negative conditions, your **Intuitive** body tends to lie dormant, which can sever your knowing-ness and awareness of much more than form shows.

In between *"on-line* and in the flow" and *"way-off-line*—in *survival* all the time," is that in-between state of being "just *off-line*." This means you are a human Being who is basically in decent shape within your Self, but you may be overly tired, overworked, financially distraught, or hit with an unexpected death of a loved one, for example, and therefore you *fluctuate* in your Re-Membering of your connected Self-expression.

Being: *(still recovering itself in light of all this new information)* I had no idea there were so many facets of my Self, being the fish in my pond.

(The Being, Unicorn, Amethyst Crystal, and Gabriella recall with a shared smile Astro's "fish in water" analogy, that a fish in water truly does not see the water it is swimming in because it is immersed in it, and does not perceive the water as separate from its Self.)

Astro: *(taking the Being's thought further)* In fact, Being, that's where the spirit of your dog Gabriella comes in as your emotional body representative, and why she is so close to you in heart. For it is in the Middle realm of the emotional member, the **Psychic-Intuitive** awareness, that many things are *get-able* to a human Being, even though the access is invisible. Unfortunately, it is not easily measurable or "grade-able," so it is not widely promoted, *experientially,* in Earth school systems as yet.

(continuing with a wry smile) I have this idea that by the turn of the century, quite possibly someone will get a Nobel Prize for discovering scientifically that what is invisible to the eye, such as Love, is more significant and grander than anything we can see. In other words, the notion will be officially recognized that the invisible is filled with endless possibility and eternal awareness. It will also be recognized that **the "invisible" is with us while we are in form, to assure a *quality* of living in such a way that miracles become common experiences and the effort of daily concerns lightens up enough for humans to move on into other creative endeavors, as opposed to spending so much time in "survival" or countering themselves energetically.**

(now looking directly at Unicorn) And last, but no less impactful, Unicorn, the aura and chakras, or **Subtle Physical Body,** consisting of vibration and energy, are directly linked to our physical health or lack thereof. Their level of functioning—or lack thereof—may even be at the basis of chronic depression and long-term debilitation. We know they exist, for we can now take pictures of a person's aura, and experientially, the chakras are "get-able" too. There may even be five or more human chakras re-emerging in our consciousness, increasing the total to at least twelve. If humanity begins to utilize all these energy centers, it might assist them all toward living consciously both in their humanity and divinity at the same time. Who knows, as I always say—and I mean it: **Anything is possible!** At the very least, these Middle bodies or levels of awareness are designed to balance one's living-ability with one's eternal nature.

Gabriella: *(beaming and hardly able to contain its Self)* I get it! Consciousness has no form and is invisible, which made it hard to learn and grow in its knowledge of itself. So, it pretended to forget it was whole in each human Being, so it could open up ways to view itself and interact with itself on many levels. And we, the body representatives, are part of the means for consciousness or Totality to communicate with our particular Being in human form. Am I right?

Astro: *(Stunned speechless, Astro gawks openly at the emotional member, hardly believing it has heard Gabriella correctly, and finally speaks.)* That's not only right, Gabriella, but it brings me to my next point. With so many perceptual viewers (in this case, human Beings), there arises a need for a system or some means of connecting all learning. I refer to this system of energy-collecting portals as six distinct "Es-

sences." And to make them get-able in Earth terms, I refer to them as "mystical magical viewing places" and give them the names **Angelic, Fairy, Elvian, Unicorn, Dwarvian,** and **Wizard.**

Amethyst Crystal: *(completely lost and frustrated)* Wait a dog-gone minute. I can sort of understand that there are expanded levels of self-expression for each of us, physically, mentally, and emotionally, but what has that got to do with these so-called *Essences?*

Astro: *(always amused at how Amethyst Crystal has to put things in chronological order, as if one bit of news always follows another)* Let me answer your question with a question of my own. Exactly what is this Being to you? Or, what is your relationship to this Being?

Amethyst Crystal: *(certain that this is a trick question, answering hesitantly)* I sort of work for her, you might say.

Astro: Exactly! Without this consciousness known as a female in form, friendly in feeling and quick in intelligence, we would be unaware of its vibrating presence. The physical body representative gives her form, the emotional body representative gives her feeling, and you, my friend, give her thinking. But what is *it*, really?

(Astro continues before Unicorn, Gabriella, or Amethyst Crystal can respond) It is *Essence.* And not all Essence views its Totality from the same angle. It's these angles, as well as you body representatives—oh, and also each Being's "base" communication doorway—that make up what I call *Humanology in Motion*™ or the ongoing study and evolvement of humanity within spirituality. Like the ancient Vedas, as they

are called on Earth, this study contains All Knowledge and has no beginning and no end.

Amethyst Crystal: You mean to say you can study something in form, without "being" in form?

Astro: *(with a chuckle)* Kind of frightening, isn't it. Once you grasp that *form* and *formless-ness* are one and the same, like *visible* and *invisible*, then none of it is separate—and it *is* study-able. And as this is where I put my focus, it makes me a practitioner of the *invisible arts*, which are what I sometimes call **Imagenetics**™. Pretty cool, huh?

Unicorn: *(astounded, and naturally gravitating to its particular concern)* Is that why many humans can't *see* unicorns anymore but still believe in them?

Astro: From the standpoint of fairy tales, that's exactly what we're talking about and why I believe that the myths of unicorns have survived through the eons of time, even though credence in them has grown less and less and less.

   (The Being gazes at its physical body representative with even more appreciation, recognizing the "energy" that it holds, of the unicorn.)

Astro: *(continually full of notions)* And since all of life is the subject of Humanology, let me put its scope in more succinct terms. **Being Human and Divine** is knowing that we are in a human body, having a human experience, but that we are not these bodies—and at the same time knowing *experientially* that anything *is* truly possible—and that we are completely in charge of how our chunk of Totality gets along in life. **Being Human and Divine** is also knowing that this body, with its thoughts and feelings, will some day pass away—leaving us not with dollar bills or a loved one or some other material gain, but instead with a sense of universal Truth and cosmic Knowingness in a beautifully orchestrated Eternity.

(The dawning of understanding begins to brighten Amethyst Crystal's purple glow and to gradually ease the frustration out of its energy field.)

Astro: *(still immersed in the topic and almost as an afterthought)* After all, as far as I can see, the emphasis on intellect and information and college degrees on Earth—although valuable to a point—on its own, has not substantially improved the *quality* of life for humanity.

Amethyst Crystal: *(jerked out of its momentary bliss)* Are you saying that human Beings, communicating through *my* doorway, are not better off than 100 years ago?

Astro: Whoa, there, A.C., it's often hard to speak in mental terms without seeming to pass judgment. What I mean by *quality of life* is the integration of that which is felt by the *Physical* and *Emotional* aspects of experiencing, as opposed to the perception of life strictly in a linear, visual fashion. As I've mentioned before, it's not about losing or lessening any one of you, but rather about linking your skills and contributions in such a way that your Being can share more of its Self.

(All the members and the Being emit a sigh of relief, and after a moment of silence they collectively arrive at the same question.)

The Being and all its members: So, Astro, what exactly are these **Essences?**

Astro: *(grinning impishly)* I thought you'd never ask.

I live my life in growing orbits
which move out over the things of the world...
I am circling around God...

—Ranier Maria Rilke, *A Book for the Hours of Prayer*

When we Re-Member our union with Oneness,
the Earthly plane aligns with us.
When we forget, we move into life's circumstances,
which are never done....
To Re-Member is to bring the members together to reach
wholeness, balance, and integration—"lest we forget."

—JL

You must be able to operate with a higher electrical current inside your
body. ... Increased energy inside yourself will activate hidden talents
and trigger a renaissance of psychic abilities: clairvoyance,
clairaudience, telepathy, and perceptual awareness that involves
"knowing" far beyond what you can currently consider. ...
You are going to climb a ladder and experience
a different view from which to interpret reality.

—Barbara Marciniak, *EARTH: Pleiadian Key to the Living Library*

CHAPTER FIVE

THE MAGICAL ESSENCES REVISITED

(Astro waits patiently as a light bulb goes off in the Being's and its members' energy fields, and they all remember that the "Magical Essences" had appeared to them briefly during their collective dream.)

Astro: *(proceeding as if they had spoken aloud)* As you are now recalling from the dream experience of Totality, there are six Magical Essences, each representing different viewing spaces of the whole: the **Angelic** Essence, which emanates the quality of *Connectedness*; the **Fairy** Essence, infused with the quality of *Lightness*; and the **Elvian** Essence, vibrating as the energy of *Mischievous Motion*. Yet another perceptual viewing space is that of the **Unicorn,** of *Profound Belief,* and a fifth aspect expresses the **Dwarvian** Essence of *Groundedness.* And finally, the sixth vibratory dynamic conveys the **Wizard** Essence of *Intensity.*

(now addressing the Being) Being, do you recall describing yourself as having an *Elvian* quality, when you tried to describe yourself last year, before we formally met?

(The Being, smiling wonderingly with a mischievous twinkle in its eye, only nods its head at its preexisting identification with the Elvian point of view.[1])

---

[1] As stated by the Being in the opening scene of *The Body Talks and I Can Hear It,* p. 14.

Amethyst Crystal: *(interrupting)* So our Being is an *Elvian* Essence?

Astro: *(teasingly)* Well ... yes, you could say so—she does at times exhibit many Elvian qualities. It's just that we are dealing with invisibility, here, as well as worldliness, and the Essence isn't always something you can put "into a box." Besides, the information isn't linear at all. So why don't you listen to what I can share about each of the six Essences or perceptual viewing spaces on Totality, and perhaps along the way you can begin to get a "holographic" idea of your Self.

(Amethyst Crystal stares penetratingly at Astro, its mental antenna snapping into high focus, wondering why the air of mystery in Astro's remarks.)

(Astro, ignoring Amethyst Crystal's intense gaze for the moment, turns to face Unicorn, who is blushing all over at the mention of its name as one of the Essences.)

Unicorn: *(sheepishly)* Would it be an interruption to say I'm a little confused at this point?

Astro: Not at all. If only the English language had more words to represent the invisible or spiritual world, we might not have this problem. And furthermore, the confusion doesn't just show up here. An overlap of terms also shows up between the distinctions of your cohorts, the mental and emotional representatives, since we use those very same words in the terms *mental base* and *emotional base,* in describing how human Beings tend toward one base or the other as a means of communicating their thoughts and feelings. Not surprisingly, if any human can sort through this overlapping of terms and come out with any clarity, it will be a wonder.

(Unicorn, a little more at ease in its confusion, looks over to see both Gabriella and Amethyst emit a sigh of relief. All the while, the Being seems suspended in pure uncertainty.)

Astro: Unicorn, let me see if I can clarify your personal confusion, and perhaps doing so will help bring the other overlapping terms into clearer focus as well. You see, not all human Beings have a Unicorn as their physical body representative—even though *Unicorn* is one of the Magical Essences. *(now turning to Amethyst Crystal)* In fact, if you recall, A.C., prior to your Being's recognizing you as the full expression of her mental body representative, you showed up for her as a Wizard—and *Wizard* is also one of the Magical Essences. **A human Being can use any image for its body members, as a means to access them individually and clear out their arenas of expression.** It just happened that your Being functions a lot on the imaginative realm, so a *Wizard* was a natural image to pop in as an initial mental body representative. **Some humans locate animals as images; some, nature; some, color; and some, vibrating energy with no form—all depending on which image shows the full attributes of the physical, mental, and emotional expressions of that particular human.**[2]

But when your Being cleared out her mental body's arena, you then appeared in your present glorious form of an *Amethyst Crystal,* giving her more access to and support from you, her mental member.

Getting back to your case, Unicorn, you started out as an image of a *Jaguar,* but when the physical body itself was cleared out, cleansed, and revamped, and the full attributes of

---

[2] Refer to *The Body Talks and I Can Hear It* to explore this method of inner self-perception.

the physical body representative were shared with your Being, the image of a *Unicorn* came to mind, with your beautiful white coat and magical horn, to represent the physical body's more encompassing attributes to her.

(addressing them all as a group) And regarding the overlap of the terms *mental* and *emotional* when referring to a Being's dense-body members as well as its base of communication, perhaps I can make the distinction more clear. Like you, Amethyst Crystal, and you, Gabriella, **each human Being has both a mental and an emotional avenue through which the Being expresses its Self, along with a physical body.** In other words, in physical form, people hear a Being's thoughts and feelings and see their body. **Yet, each human expresses through either the** *emotional* **doorway or base, or the** *mental* **doorway or base, as a means of speaking the Self.**

The *emotional* base of communication shows up as a leaning toward using language expressions such as, "*I* see this...," "*I'm* experiencing this feeling...," or "*I* have difficulty with what's going on,"—rather than "Stop irritating me!" "Look how unusual *that* person dresses," "*You've* just got to do such and so," or "*You* really should consider getting a new car—after all, *yours* breaks down so often"—which would be the *mentally-based* way of stating things.

Can you hear the difference? It's the difference between speaking the Self from within, as the *emotional base*, or speaking the Self while focused on an outer-directed view, as the *mental base*. And neither is good or bad, better or worse, but rather a dichotomy of human expression.

(Gabriella, sensing the enormity of this concept for its Being and its colleagues Amethyst Crystal and Unicorn, as well as

for all of humanity, gently and lovingly approaches the topic to check its grasp of Astro's communication.)

Gabriella: What you've just shared, Astro, is a very impactful notion. I sense that what you're trying to tell us is this: even though Unicorn is our physical body representative, the *Unicorn Essence* is not limited to just our domain, but rather it's a perceptual viewing place that many human Beings hold, from what you are calling either a *mental* or an *emotional base of communication.* And you also seem to be saying that whatever Essence a Being is, if they primarily uses the "I" word to express themselves, they are *emotionally-based,* and if they primarily refer to others in their speech, they have the *mental base* of communication. Is this anywhere in the realm of this *Humanology* you speak of?

Astro: *(in peace and contentment)* Not only *in* the realm, it *is* it.

The Being: *(grateful for Gabriella's comprehension and clear statement of this study of humanity within spirituality, and thoroughly intrigued with the doorway that Astro has just opened a crack of)* So, Astro, what else can you tell us about all these *Essences?* I have to admit that during what I thought was my dream, I didn't pay full attention to all of those perceptual viewing places you spoke of. I mean, we aren't talking *archetypes,* here, are we?

Astro: *(pausing pensively)* The initial answer to your question, Being, is *no,* for we are all of the One-ness, which means that *every* conceivable viewing place is within *all* human Beings. And yet, as I've said, a person tends to *lean toward* a viewing place, within the Magical Essence spectrum, which might seem like an archetype. However, archetypes, which indicate that something is *this* and not *that,* can be visible, whereas

Magical Essences, emanating from the invisible realm, are mostly "get-able." For our purposes, in the magical realm, we are going to say there are just six viewing places, each with two communication doorways, making twelve general perceptual spaces in all. Yet, each individual expression of that viewing place and doorway will be quite unique, depending on the individual's point of view, history, lessons, and talents.

(Astro stops a moment to locate a familiar example.)

Astro: Remember when we connected at last year's Symposium, I spoke of humanity as if it were a bicycle wheel, with each human Being having their particular point of view, like a spoke on the wheel. At the very same time, all spokes by design lead to the wholeness at the center in order for the wheel to work. In actuality, not the image of a *three-dimensional wheel* but rather a *multidimensional hologram* more appropriately expresses humanity's connection to its Self and the Cosmos. I'm simply using these Magical Essences as a way to engage in the conversation of this hologram.

Unicorn: *(in a new quandary)* So how does someone "get" their Essence, if it isn't form, and if every trait really is in everybody?

Astro: Good question—especially since we know that we are not referring to personality, and yet someone's personality can reflect the nature of their Essence. Then, certain physical presentations also tend to hold true or give a clue to some people's leanings. For example, **Angelic** folks (both men and women) tend to have a fullness of body. We see it as the hourglass figure in women and as a soft feel to the skin and a little extra weight for the male. The **Fairy** Essence leans toward the very slender and not too terribly tall. The **Elvian** may also be lean and a little taller than the Fairy, and particularly with a shorter upper body, often with longer legs. The **Unicorn** is again a fuller, taller figure, often with a larger bone structure, and women may have a full head of hair—which may be worn in a pony tail at some time in life. The men are good-looking and even have a softness about them, no matter which base of communication they speak from or how strong they are. The **Dwarvian** Essence often appears well-balanced in proportions, having a long upper body with shorter legs, or equidistant both upward and downward from the waist. The Dwarvians tend to have a solid-ness about them, both men and women, whether they exercise or not. Lastly, by the very nature of the **Wizard**'s shape-shifting activity, it is hard to pin down the physical form or any attribute of this Essence, except for its basic *modus operandi,* that is, its *intensity*—whether expressing enthusiasm or upset.

Again, these are just tendencies and clues to locating a person's viewing place. And even if you have an idea of someone's perceptual view, other traits will make the Essence more get-able. For example, ask yourself if someone is mischievous, or intense, or light and nonconfrontive, or steady, or sensitive, or very loving. Even though we all exude *some* of these traits from time to time, some people exude *one* of these traits a great deal of the time.

Amethyst Crystal: So, Astro, why the "magical" terms, if it doesn't refer to the forms associated with fairy tale characters?

Astro: *(appreciative of the question)* Actually, the fairy tale characters originate from the Essences themselves, A.C., for even though they are invisible, an awareness in consciousness of each perceptual viewing space has filtered down through the eons of timelessness and human history, and has survived somewhat in our mythology and fairy tales. However, only the barest minimum of the fullness of each Essence has been preserved in our known fairy tales, myths, and legends. In fact, from this point forward in our conversation, you may need to remind yourselves not to fall into the habit of confusing these Mystical Magical Essences with their limited earthly-conceived popular forms. For that, you can go to Disneyland, U.S.A. For, it is the *Essence* of the magical natures, not their *form*, that we are interested in exploring. And, as you saw in the dream, Essence has a *direct* link to all of Totality—just as all you members do through your expanded levels—even though you happen to be viewing Totality from this particular vantage point, your human form.

(Amethyst Crystal, enthralled with all this information, spontaneously jumps out of its nonskin as it remembers an earlier thought.)

Amethyst Crystal: *(appearing to interrupt the conversation)* So is our Being really an *Elvian* essence?

Astro: *(with a knowing smile)* Well, why don't I give you more information about each Essence—and then *you* can tell me.

We are here on Planet Earth to see the many as One,
as well as the One representing the many,
as a living example of the wholeness we all are.

—Cathy Sechrist

At the cosmic scale,
The impossible has possibilities of being true.

—Teilhard de Chardin

♡ CHAPTER SIX ♡

THE ANGELIC ESSENCE

Glowing Connectors — "They give so they can live."

Astro: *(settling in to the most knowable of the Magical Essences, as experienced on the Earth plane)* Those humans who express the **Angelic** Essence can be called **Earth's Glowing Connectors,** for the **Angelics** literally connect Heaven and Earth by their presence. In fact, the **Angelics'** gift in life is that they are connected, and extremely so, to everything within their awareness, and they absolutely "hold the space" of *connection* and *connect-ability* for all humanity. As a result, they are extremely connected to and present with "family" or a sense of family, and not just the biological folk! For **Angelics** are connected to the conversation they're having, the people they're with, and the events that surround them. Regardless of what activity they're engaged in, their presence and awareness connects Heaven and Earth, self and others, Self with God as God, and so on. They function in and as the channel that bridges the wholeness of spirituality or "All That Is" with our individual perceptions or "human Being-ness" and earthly lessons.

Angelics exude **Love and Connected-ness**; this loving and caring quality seems just to ooze from all their pores, causing them to emanate an aura of comfort, so it is not surprising that everyone tends to feel comfortable in the presence of the

Angelic Essence. When **on-line** within themselves, the **Angelics** just seem to glow with Love from the inside, as if lit up by a huge ball-like furnace of Light that radiates outward to bathe everyone around them in its healing glow.

Astro: *(warming to the topic and ignoring a signal from Amethyst Crystal, who wants to interrupt)* Because of this quality, the **Angelics** often serve as "energy boosters" to all those who are within their radius of influence, which is why they are sometimes at risk of others "plugging in" to them and "filling their tanks" at the expense of the **Angelics'** energy reserves. Unfortunately, with all the uncertainty, fear, and strife on Earth, there are quite a few "drained" **Angelics** nowadays, as a result of so many folks looking to them for reassurance and comfort. And, true to their nature, the **Angelics** respond by giving away "chunks" of themselves, as well as their time, finances, expertise, and energy. In fact, a key phrase for the **Angelics** is, *They give so they can live.* For, the **Angelics,** above all other Essences, *cannot* be moved off their aware- ness of wholeness—which means they know the natural flow of Love and sometimes have little patience for others who do not seem to aspire to their own highest good.

They can also sit in the midst of extremely upsetting circum- stances and surroundings—and at times many of them have "sat" with tremendous upsets and abuses and managed to survive out of their solid knowingness of Love in the heart. All the while, they somehow maintain the God-connection, even though they are scared, sad, exhausted, or lonely. Out of all the Essences, the **Angelic** *knows,* really knows, we're all connected, despite the seeming *disparancies,*[1] disbeliefs, and

---

[1] That is, appearances of separate-ness.

distresses of the world and its endless uncertainties and changing circumstances. The **Angelics** take this awareness of connectedness everywhere they go, and they particularly feel it with small children, who are newly-arrived to the planet and still strongly aware of their universal link. And they *know,* no matter what, that all the off-kiltered-ness is *not* "us"—not our true nature, not our truth, not me, not you, not real.

(Amethyst Crystal frantically waves its energy arms to catch Astro's attention, but to no avail, as Astro sits further back on its haunches and continues its stream of aspects of the Angelic Essence.)

Also, no matter what careers the **Angelics** are interested in, people *matter* to them, because they just *are* that energy, and they want everyone to be loved, appreciated, and included.

Having wings, the **Angelics** have the ability to be "above it all"—exuding the "love essence" and liking to *bask* in this element, being joy-filled, sparkling, light-filled, and support-ive. This ability to "fly" allows them to "see the overview" of situations, while their powerful willfulness allows them to spread a **base of power** all around themselves, especially spiritual power, by virtue of their connectedness. For the Angelic, no one and no thing doesn't "fit in" somewhere, and the Angelic may be known for **always remembering and including everyone**—and in just the perfect way—whether it be at Christmas when giving gifts, or in standing up for and defending those who may have been forgotten or downtrod-den by others.

In fact, it is one of the **Angelics'** gifts to be able to speak up for or remind us all of the Truth in a powerful yet gentle way, if necessary, because they know so deeply what the Truth is. Being in direct communication with the Whole, they simply radiate that knowingness for all the rest of us, when they are *on-line* within themselves.

(Astro stops for a cosmic breath, beaming from ear to ear, totally lost in its reminiscences of this particular viewing place. Taking advantage of the pause, Amethyst Crystal blurts out its pent-up thoughts.)

Amethyst Crystal: There you go again, Astro, referring to some sort of *on-line* business. I mean I hear what you are saying about the gist of this Angelic viewing place, but what happens if a human Being holding this particular perception is not *on-line*? And just what is *on-line,* anyway?

Astro: *(jarred from its peaceful place)* Oh, yes, quite. Well, let's see. I do forget that my vocabulary is of my own making! Please forgive me, A.C.—and all of you.

(Astro notices that Unicorn, Gabriella, and the Being appear to be in a state of shock or daze of sorts, as they don't seem to respond.)

Astro: What I mean by *on-line* is what you might call **balanced, in-synch, flowing—in tune** with Nature and Magic, or **connected** with Earth and the Heavens—and not leaning toward pronouncing a particular way for people to behave. When a Being is *on-line* with its Self, its energy is contained within its Self, and it has an active interest in its own growth. This doesn't mean the Being doesn't watch others and interact, but its tendency is to take those experiences and pull them into its Self for evaluation, storage, or sharing with others, rather than to focus on how others are doing.

(Seeming to lose its place, Astro looks over to Amethyst Crystal for assistance.)

Amethyst Crystal: *(responding immediately, as it has been paying close attention to the line of explanation)* That's fine, but what if someone is not in balance, in synch. What then?

(A recognition or light bulb seems to go off in Astro's internal viewing screen.)

Astro: *(gratefully recovering its stream of thought)* Thanks, A.C. In my vocabulary—I refer to folks as being **on-line, off-line,** or **way-off-line.** For example, with this Essence, the **Angelics,** when they are *off-line* or as I affectionately say, *at-a-tilt (Astro chuckles at its own joke)*, they appear to be what on Earth is termed *self-righteous.* After all, no matter where they lean to, they know deep in their heart that all is connected, so when they get tired, overworked, or overwrought with the number of people relying on them, they can sometimes respond by sounding "holier than thou" or judging other people's conduct or behavior. It comes across kind of like "they know all"—indicating that others don't—and that *their* way is *the* way.

For it is when we move out of our connectedness and awareness of "all as one" that we (and by *we*, I mean any of the Essences) begin to judge the world from just "our" particularly vantage point. For the **Angelics,** the judgment reaction may tend to center around moral issues and the use by others of foul language, which is like fingernails on a blackboard to an at-a-tilt **Angelic.** Quite frankly, **Angelics** are never fond of foul language, but when they are way out-of-whack, or *way-off-line,* they may start using those words themselves. More frequently, though, the *way-off-line* **Angelics** lean towards martyrdom (if they come through the mental doorway) or victimhood (those of the emotional doorway), depending on their base of communications.

(Astro, looking over to see how Amethyst Crystal is receiving this bit of news—for it could easily sound a bit judgmental—and sees that A.C. seems to be accepting the information without hesitation.)

Astro: *(returning to the flow)* The **Angelics** are powerfully magnetic as well. Because of their connectedness to all things, they may tend to stay within their own physical realm, such as their home, workplace, or the like, and magnetically seem to *draw* to themselves the resources they require. They are transmutors of energy and powerful *be*-ers, having a knack for just sitting back and letting things and people come to them.

In the business world, they may have less of a need than other folks to go out into the world and make connections and promote themselves, for even if they stay home—people, opportunities, and resources will seek out and find the **Angelics.** Of course, when enthused, they also like to go out into the world and share their loving nature. It's just that the **Angelic** may, simply by putting out a notion into the universe or "speaking its word," attract what it wants and needs.

Likewise, when it comes to physical exercise, the **Angelic** may gravitate more toward the flowing or connected expression of dancing rather than strictly cardiovascular or weight-machine workouts. Or they may gain the benefits of exercise through the walking about during shopping, housekeeping, or running errands, as a part of the flow of life, rather than engaging in exercise for exercise's sake—unless of course it is their passion—for instance, snow skiing. In that case, they will be quite at home on the slopes.

As parents, **Angelics** may gravitate strongly toward babies, and they may find themselves extremely fertile on the Earth plane when the heartfelt connectedness of physical love occurs. Likewise, because of their connectedness to all things, they may bring home "strays"—both human and animal. In fact, they are less likely than others to lean toward divorce, unless the marriage really is detrimental to their health.

The **Angelics'** heartfelt expression is evident when they seek to connect with others, for they are inward-directed, in terms of valuing inner truths, and they like to "get to the *heart* of the matter" rather than engage in shallow conversation. Similarly, they tend not to want to lose connections with people or for others to "flit away" from them. They are the world's great includers.

Of all the Essences, the Angelics hold the strongest sense of heart-related matters and are most confident in backing others' skills and possibilities. Especially when they are clear in this purpose, they love being out in the world, knowing they are helping it to be a better place by helping others.

Gabriella: *(who has been listening intently, wonders out loud)* Excuse me, Astro, but this Angelic Essence seems to reflect my arena a lot. After all, I am the means of communication for a human Being to share its love. Is this somehow related to being "emotionally-based"?

(Again amazed at the depth of the emotional member's profound grasp of the almost ungraspable, Astro sees that it

is timely to restate the distinctions between the emotional and mental bases and the individuals' mental and emotional members.)

Astro: I can see from your question, Gabriella, that you "get" what I am talking about, and I would be happy to clarify it further. You see, each Essence, as it comes into form, has the nine known avenues that we discussed earlier, to express its "Self"—the three densest represented in your Being's case by you, Unicorn, and A.C. And at the very same time, the Earth plane functions in a dichotomy, like two ends of the same stick, for each Essence, linking both the cosmic and human nature through these nine known systems. But over the eons of *in-form-ness*, each Being has managed to lean to a specific way of making that communication, and I call that being *mentally* or *emotionally* based.

It's what comes out of a person's mouth that I am referring to. Some people, the **mentally-based,** are constantly looking outside themselves to see themselves, with thoughts spoken such as, "Did *you* see the game today—what did *you* think?" or "If only *you* would clean up after yourself, I wouldn't be late to my gym class from picking up after you."

On the other hand, an **emotionally-based** person will tend to speak from within itself, saying, "*I'm* so exhausted. *I* really had a great game of golf today," or "*I* am so sorry, *I* can't remember if our date is tonight, or is it tomorrow night?" *(Astro looks apologetic.)* I know that is a long and partly redundant answer to a short question, but the point is that **even though the Angelic Essence is "love and connection" oriented, the way to "speak" or express that Essence can be either from an emotional or a mental communication base.** Does that make sense, Gabriella?

(Gabriella, "eyes" twinkling in understanding, acknowledges with a nod of its "head.")

Astro: *(pausing only a moment to regain its thoughts)* **Angelics,** being the connection between heaven or Totality and Earth or the individual expression of the Totality, are naturally inclined toward prayer and meditation as a means of strengthening the connection to the whole, on behalf not only of themselves but all of humanity. For they also experience most literally a sense of carrying and feeling deeply all the ills of the world in their hearts! Everyone's pain is their pain.

Many **Angelics** are experiencing great trouble on Earth right now, because humans are in the very midst of the change from isolation to connectivity, vulnerability, and letting people in, whereas most people have been taught to avoid failure, keep up appearances, avoid getting hurt or being vulnerable, and so on. **The Angelics *know* and *help us know* that no matter how we mess up, or *do* life, we *are* connected to wholeness, God, and magic—and therefore, our *value* is a given.** Eventually, the sense of "disconnectedness" on Earth will disappear, but meanwhile, most of humanity has been operating from the orientation of being "self-sufficient" or "lone ducks in a pond" rather than "cooperative through community." As a result, people flock to the **Angelics** and siphon them, without realizing what they are doing.

So, even though the **Angelics** tend to hold the space of wholeness, they may not be having the best time of it. It's natural for those operating in "separation mode," like moths in the darkness, to be attracted to the flaming light within the **Angelics,** for most **Angelics** are lit up with love and appreciation, like lighthouses, like beacons in the darkness. **And just as we're attracted to the brilliant flame of a candle in the**

darkness, we're attracted to the Angelics and take comfort in their glow.... However, in the process, we run the risk of extinguishing the light!

The Being: *(with sudden tears in its eyes)* May I ask a question here?

Astro: *(noting the Being's prolonged quietness)* Of course, Being, you have been so quiet.

The Being: I'm a little concerned about what you just said about extinguishing the Angelics' light. I feel like you just struck such a chord inside me.

Astro: Could this possibly be some sense of your Self?

The Being: So I'm really an **Angelic Essence**?

Astro: *(with a mysterious nod)* Remember, we still have five Essences to go, and we're not done yet with this one. *(Astro pauses for effect before continuing.)* Many of the **Angelics** are in need of support, because their tanks have been running a bit low. Some **Angelics** have even found it necessary to retreat from the world at large, at least temporarily, and some have actually broken down physically from all they have absorbed of the world's ills. However, even though it may seem the darkest that it ever has for the **Angelics,** it is the darkness before the dawn breaks, for the shift into awareness of connectedness is occurring even as we speak. But even that knowledge may not be too comforting to the **Angelics'** current distress, for humans are still engaged in the unsettling shift from a place of *dis-connectedness* into the awareness and acceptance of our wholeness. **Let's just remember that we all get a healing as we give one, and no one knows this any better than the Angelic Essence.**

Amethyst Crystal: But can we tell by looking at an Angelic whether we're seeing one?

Astro: In the physical presentation, as we mentioned before, **Angelics** tend to have a curvy, tending-to-voluptuous shape—not necessarily heavy, but their curves are evident. The attractive, magnetic quality and the love "oozing" from their pores is also "feel-able." Surely you can call to mind many examples, once you begin to think of the people you know.

Unicorn: *(its interest piqued by the connection of Essence to form)* Hey, Astro, I thought you said that we were talking about the invisible realm?

Astro: *(chuckling under its breath)* Don't suppose I can get much past you alert body members, can I? *(still chuckling at the change in this Being's body representatives)* You're right, of course, Unicorn; I am talking about the invisible nature of vibration and energy. However, if I haven't mentioned it before, this invisible factor is what's behind all that you see in the third-dimensional world you are currently involved in.

     (Unicorn and Amethyst Crystal turn towards each other, then look questioningly at Astro. Seeing their confusion, Astro continues.)

Astro: Let me say this another way. When I speak of *Essence* and *Being-ness* and the *Oneness*, I am really talking about the same thing, but in different stages of development. In the beginning, of which there is no measurement, there is Oneness—the Whole—call it Consciousness, Everything/Nothing/the Void/God/the Indefinable. Prior to form, there are many, many stages of unfoldment, but for the sake of time, let's say that with enough awareness and vibration, Oneness moves into Essence.

     And when *Essence* and *Vibration* continue with *Energy*, we have individual *Being-ness* that shows up in *Form*, through body representatives such as you—bearing in mind that we now know of at least nine versions of communicating this Being-ness, of which you three systems are the densest or most visible, in form.

And truly, most humans don't even see their mental member, A.C., or their emotional member, Gabriella, but they feel and "get" you as though they do. And some people do physically see auras or thoughts or dreams or vital force energy, which says to me that people are starting to *Re-Member* themselves—as I said earlier—on more levels or dimensions. Does that help you understand, Unicorn?

(As Unicorn ponders Astro's restatement of these notions, a light bulb goes off inside its vibration.)

Unicorn: I believe I am beginning to grasp what you are repeating to us, Astro, or maybe where you are heading. You are saying that *form* is what we see, but what we see is a kind of culmination of information from *all* these means of communicating the experience of one chunk of consciousness known as a human Being. And human form can radiate this information?

(As Unicorn is speaking, Amethyst Crystal gets a crystallized awareness that a person's body form can show something that isn't *"form.")*

(Once again Astro realizes the tremendous shifts in thought, get-ability, and possibility in this Being and its densest body representatives and, after a moment or so, returns to the conversation at hand.)

Astro: That is very astute, Unicorn. In fact, you can see this visible aspect of interconnectedness in the way that **Angelics,** for example, tend to choose clothes and decorate their homes, as they may very well gravitate towards "heavenly" colors, often showing a definite preference for white and gold, or they may seek out rosy pinks, comforting greens, gold-tinged oranges, and the light blue of the sky.

And whether the **Angelics** lean toward a refined sense of place and harmony or toward function-ability, the comfort and welcome of their homes will be a given. This sense, plus their ability to operate from a full base of power with a gentle delivery, may find them engaged in merchandising, as in creating, decorating, and running a retail store, or serving in a profession that emphasizes "connectedness" in some way—human resources, for example, or real estate. If they are in real estate, they won't just sell homes—they'll create communities.

Similarly, their ability to hold the Heaven-Earth connection enables many **Angelics** to be not only excellent parents, but also to engage in the healing professions, not the least due to their innate ability to "sit with" others' pain and hold open the connection to wholeness for those who are suffering. Also because of their unique ability to maintain a perspective of wholeness during adverse situations, it is not surprising to find many **Angelics** who have been injured or "handicapped" in one way or another, and whose lives serve as examples and inspirations to others.

*(As Astro comes out of its soliloquy, it notices a profound shift in the expressions of all three dense body representatives and the Being as well, as if a whole new world has opened before them. Astro then begins to formulate information on a much lighter, yet no less powerful Essence—the **Fairy**.)*

In "Love," the Heart gallops,
and desperately the Head hangs on.

—Tom White

I will not wish thee riches, nor the glow of greatness,
but that wherever thou go some weary heart shall gladden at thy smile,
or shadowed life know sunshine for a while.
And so thy path shall be a track of light,
like angels' footsteps passing through the night.

—words on a church wall in Upwaltham, England

But I have learned that all you give is all you get,
*So **give it all you've got.***

—from the song "Here's to You," sung by David Masenheimer
(emphasis added)

You cannot look at one single of our global problems in isolation,
trying to understand it and solve it. Of course, you can
fix a fragment or a piece, but it will deteriorate a second later,
because what it is connected to has been ignored.

—*Mindwalk* (based on Fritzof Capra, *The Tao of Physics*)

There is Total Oneness, and in this Oneness we speak the Word.
Let the sense of separation be dissolved.
Let mankind be returned to Godkind.

—World Healing Meditation, Planetary Commission for Global Healing

CHAPTER SEVEN

THE FAIRY ESSENCE

When a Fairy takes flight, we all receive Light.
With a Fairy on the wing—all Hearts sing.

Astro: The second of the heavenly Essences is literally *all* **Lightness**. This is the **Star-Studded Messenger of the Cosmos**— the **Fairy Essence**. Like the **Angelics, Fairy** folk have "wings" and can rise above all the density on Earth, but unlike the **Angelics,** these "winged" energies are not grounded— they are in fact starbound as opposed to earthbound, being in and of the cosmos, and very little of the Earth. Whereas **Angelics** are both Heaven-bound and Earth-bound, serving as the Connectedness of All That Is, the **Fairy** perceptual viewing place makes these humans **the natural messengers of Totality and the Keepers of the Rainbow.** In this capacity, **they literally light the way for the rest of us, bringing light to the darkness, joy to our hearts, and God's Radiant Being or Wholeness to each aspect of the whole.**

The **Fairy Essence,** physically speaking, often shows up in a human body frame as small-boned or even tiny, with their top height rarely being more than 5 feet 6 inches or so, while being thin and lithe-full. Occasionally one may run across a tall **Fairy Essence,** but usually they have a smaller bone structure than other humans. At the same time, they appear to be not as affected by gravity as others and often look younger than their age. Simply because they may be tinier is not to say that their presence is insignificant, for their cosmic role is huge, as were their original wingspans.

Male or female, the **Fairy Essence** emanates as **light, lightness, sparkle, play,** and **motion. Fairies** tend to be—and gravitate to that which is—shiny, glittery, quick, bubbly, and non-serious. Having an effervescent *whee!* of a time and getting a message out are very much in their natural domain—as long as they don't have to be *too* realistic (by Earth's standards), because they don't like to take this place (planet Earth) so seriously. They are not here to explain, convince, or defend any bit of news, but are simply great at getting the word broadcast.

Their "glow-in-the-dark" energy is designed to raise the vibrations of the planet. Unfortunately, since much of humanity is denser than they are, those of the **Fairy Essence** may not be "heard" or "received" as significant contributors to a project or relationship—and hence their lack or appearance of lack of interest in a particular project or another person. **This Essence is definitely the lightest energy, and the Fairy Essence is *very* sensitive and finely-tuned to its surroundings.** If anyone appears to be "out in the clouds," it is this Essence.

(Gabriella, feeling the effects of Astro's statements, visibly shudders, which gets Astro's attention.)

Astro: I see that what I have said has impacted you, Gabriella. Do you mind sharing your feelings with us?

(Gabriella, a bit startled that Astro had read its exact awareness, willingly complies.)

Gabriella: Well, I guess I was feeling that business about *isolation* and *separateness,* and just maybe why these Fairy Essences appear sometimes to be uninterested in the activities or people around them. I mean, if someone was sharing their natural buoyant enthusiasm, and others didn't even acknowledge it or ignored their comments or judged them—I don't believe such a response would encourage a Being to share themselves again. Especially if they are as *sensitive* as you say. In fact, it would really hurt me—and does sometimes.

(Astro ponders Gabriella's feelings while Unicorn comes over and gives Gabriella a big hug.)

Astro: Definitely food for thought, Gabriella. Putting it in **Fairy** rhyme,

I can see you are all beginning to see,
How deadly words or actions can be,
If thrown around haphazardly.

(A chuckle is heard from every member at the whimsical, rhythmical statement.)

Astro: *(in tune with its lighter nature)* As the Keepers of the Light, the **Fairy Essence** holds the space on the planet for Lightness, Enlightenment, and Lightening-Up. Besides being highly visible, the Fairy Essence is extremely mobile and helps keep humanity from becoming too stagnant. They love spontaneity, adventure, and changing directions. As the personification of Lightness itself, those who view life from the **Fairy** perspective simply cannot imagine that there are some folks who do not want to keep dancing about and playing!

Fairy folks tend to run in groups—like fireflies or butterflies—and if you know a **Fairy Essence,** quite likely they have lots and lots of **Fairy** or at least other playful friends, with whom they can jibber-jabber endlessly, talking *very* fast when they get excited and even over each other, or whiling away the time in pursuits that to others might seem silly or pointless. Talking fast and all over each other doesn't bother the **Fairy** folk, if emotionally-based, because they can do that and still get the gist of what's being "transmitted" by the other, without having to hear every word. When feeling its oats, the **Fairy Essence** talks fast, and even when quiet, can offset gravity—and will never harm or bother others. These people are totally harmless, like butterflies. You will never feel like you have to push a **Fairy** energy away, it's so light. They stay high—aflight—hovering above the leaf of life rather than sitting on it.

Sometimes the **Fairy Essence** seems to know just *everyone*. "After all," they might say, "it's *such* a small world!..." And, if they seem to have trouble being serious about things, just know that in order to do their "work" of lightening the load, inspiring, enlightening, and uplifting all of humanity, their wings *must* remain unencumbered and free to maneuver quickly out of the way of heaviness—which is why they're a natural opposite, as a viewing space, from the very grounded **Dwarvian Essence.**

When the **Fairy** folks' wings are operating fully, they have a natural overview to life, which does not mean they cannot hold down a job, raise children, and carry out any work of their own choosing. The key, for them, is for that work to be lighthearted and of playful interest to them, and if they are supported fully in their lightness, they can make any work seem *so-o-o-o* easy, to boot. Unfortunately, if they should find themselves in a suppressive situation or relationship, this lighthearted, playful nature can be squelched, and the **Fairy Essence** will appear to disappear before our very eyes.

They are extremely sharp and intelligent, no matter which base of communication they speak from, for they are very quick to learn a skill or "get" an idea, if they focus just a little or simply feel one with it. But their nature is one that touches down on Earth for only brief, light moments. And without this lightness to offset gravity, indeed the world might collapse into itself from all the heaviness of its worries and concerns.

(Amethyst Crystal quickly jumps in to ask a question, before Astro can take a cosmic breath and continue.)

Amethyst Crystal: *(intrigued by this last notion)* So how exactly does the Fairy Essence keep the world afloat?

Astro: I want to commend you, A.C., on your listen-ability. Although some people might consider these folks inconsequential, in truth, it is their sparkling brightness and brilliant rainbow color that reminds all of us of the beauty of life.

Unicorn: *(jumping in with its thoughts)* So is there an *off-line* or *way-off-line* aspect to this Essence as well—or was that just the Angelic nature?

Astro: *(chuckling)* As usual, those thoughts were on the tip of my awareness. You just caught me before I could give you some examples. As I was about to say, the **Fairy Essence** is somewhat fragile by current Earth standards, lacking the stamina of some of the other viewing places. And, as their wings get clipped, so to speak, they fly closer and closer to the Earth plane, until their ability to fly seems to leave them, and they are left virtually unprotected from judgment and the feeling that occurs when someone withholds their love from them. If you recall, I mentioned to you at last year's Symposium that there is a commandment greater than the ten very profound ones many humans are already familiar with, and that commandment is, *Thou shalt not withhold Thy Self.* This refers to the situation when anyone whom we are close to, doesn't like what we said or how we acted or how we presented our Self, and they pull back the connecting factor called Love, which we are all designed to stream a non-ending abundant flow of through our Hearts. We can protect our vulnerability from those we do not know, but once we have opened our Hearts to someone or something, their withdrawal is sometimes simply too painful to bear.

Hence, people develop a Self-protective tendency to focus on the visible world and on energy "outside" the Self. It's just that for the **Fairy Essence,** this "loss of love" or withholding of Self can be devastating to their presently fragile nature.

(Pausing to catch up with its Self, Astro gets to the issue at hand.)

Astro: For example, *off-line* **Fairy Essences** may be less mothering or parenting-oriented with their children and may want to spend most of their energy on themselves. Or, they may agree with someone to their face, and then seem to go off in an entirely different direction when not with that person. Also—and this is true to some extent for all the Essences, when *off-line,* they may simply not contact another person for a long time or return their phone calls—literally deleting someone, for a length of time, from their lives. If *way-off-line,* a **Fairy** may "bolt" from family and responsibilities and appear totally uncaring and selfish.

Amethyst Crystal: *(in disbelief)* You mean to say that after receiving this pain of separation—they go and make the gap wider?

Astro: You might say it that way. Or another way to say it is that *off-line* or *way-off-line* perceptions and reactions tend to compound the situation—and this again goes for all the Essences, as each has their own version of out-of-whackness. Mentally, the separation gets compounded by pointing the finger at the "guilty party" (the person who removed their love) or emotionally, by blaming oneself for the riff (*e.g.*, "I'm not worthy to be your Mother....").

Either way, it seems to produce a similar result, which is where two people who used to genuinely like each other and knew they loved each other, now sort of believe that they don't—*as if Love can go away just because a human Being doesn't run their life the way another thinks they should.* And the **Fairy Essence** tends to be the first to bolt if an opportunity presents itself. And they tend to do it without anyone watching.

(Amethyst Crystal, Gabriella, and Unicorn, each in their own thoughts identify with having virtually enacted similar kinds of "separation" dramas to their own Being, without even realizing it. Meanwhile, Astro notes the Self-awareness within each of the body representatives as they remember their own separate-ness when they met Astro at last year's Annual Symposium of Human Body Parts. Meanwhile, the Being is formulating a notion of its own.)

Being: Astro, you keep saying, "All is Oneness," and then you give us all of these different definitions of Oneness. Is that what you are getting at with these Essences or viewing places?

That each person truly is a unique expression of the whole of the Universe through a graspable perceiving place?

Astro: *(quite delighted)* Yes, Being. You are a chunk or section of this whole universal Oneness, and within you is access to the whole Universe, yet in any given lifetime you come in with certain gifts, talents, and skills to share with other chunks or sections of the Universe, as you learn about your One-ness from your own niche.

(warming to the topic even more) If I speak to the Essence of **Fairy-ness** in terms of a spiral, when the spiral goes down to a point of separateness, heavy laden with gravity, serious-ness, and judgments, life becomes a struggle for the **Fairy Essence.** You see, **struggle is an isolated, fear-based energy drain, whereas natural enthusiasm is a cooperative venture. And when the downward spiral gets reversed by just one person, building on itself through Self-worth, passion for living, and play—and it includes others' value, joy of living, and enthusiasm—the spiral can get so huge that all involved get uplifted, and no one gets left out.**

And *this* is the gist of the Fairy Essence. When they "light down," even for just a moment, they brighten all around them, giving light to the dark and despairing, and hope to the downtrodden. To me, that is a priceless gift, and one to be acknowledged, honored, and supported. So, when looking for the **Fairy Essence,** think of those who glitter and shine: dancers, cheerleaders, models, media stars, jockeys—the key is a lightness of spirit, a certain light-bearing, lighter-than-air quality, brightness, sociability, and quickness. **"Effortless and easy"** is the signature of the **Fairy** folks. They *are* the Light that others see and are inspired by, emanating sparkle, rainbows, starriness, color, and joy. And they *love* to dance!

So if **Fairy** folk have a job to do on Earth, it is to see that the "word" gets distributed—through joy-filled movement. They are excited messengers, happily delivering the good news!

It is critically important not to *force* the **Fairy Essence** to be grounded; to do so will drain their life force away, in effect deflating their helium balloon. Again, they thrive when allowed to flit about, to flutter in like a butterfly and light down of their own volition, as well as flutter away at will. At the same time, because of their unconcern with groundedness, they can appear—and are—flighty and can also seem fickle. As with all Essences, one must check the moment's circumstances to determine if the current experience is beneficial or not, for both ends of the duality of Life can look identical in form. In other words, be sure to consider whether someone is being "fickle and flighty"—or whether a **Fairy Essence** isn't simply using its natural ability to literally **fly** *quickly* out of the way of potentially harmful energy. For any Essence, an identical action may indicate either its natural talents or its *out-of-whackness,* depending on the situation.

The **Fairy Essence** is also extremely sensitive and nonconfrontive—not quite as sensitive as the **Unicorn**—but so sensitive, in fact, that to look at them wrong could cause them to buckle—and the offender might not even know what it was they said or did. **Fairy Essences** absolutely hate discord, and a **Fairy**'s idea of a major confrontation with the boss might well be to write a letter and put it on the boss's desk at 5:00 p.m. on Friday before going on vacation, then hope that the situation gets resolved completely before they get back to work.

Astro: *(so tickled with its Self on this Essence)* The **emotionally-based Fairy** tends to take things personally and can be panic-ridden at times, if not allowed to both light down on Earth and fly away at will. If their wings are clipped or torn, their light of life diminishes, and entrapment may cause extreme panic, or in the worst-case scenario, they become as the walking dead, for without their freedom to *Be the Light,* there's little to hold the **Fairy Essence** onto the Earth plane. For their part, the **mentally-based Fairy** will be quick to agree and present a buoyant front, even when they are dying inside.

Because the **Fairy Essence** may at times have had trouble being "heard" or "taken seriously," they may appear to have trouble "doing" or "saying" things out loud—especially to a person they are out of sorts with. This tendency for others to overlook or disregard the contribution of this Essence may stem in part from the fact that they make their point in such a light unassuming way, or it may arise from the generally popular belief that **Fairy** energy is as insignificant-sized as Tinkerbell or a firefly. Remember that originally, when **Fairy** folks first appeared in Essence on a cosmic level, they were immense Light-filled Beings with huge powerful wingspans. Unfortunately, there is a tendency among the rest of humanity not to take the **Fairy Essence** seriously and to discount the things the **Fairy** is excited about, and sometimes only to half-listen to what they are eager to share. But after all, everyone deserves to be "heard," including these whimsical delightful Beings.

The **Fairy** folk do love to hear about goings on, and they like to watch the mischief that an **Elvian** Essence might create— but only from the edge of the excitement, not necessarily to perpetrate it. They live the adventuresome aspects of life somewhat vicariously, and when participating may appear thoughtless, without regard for the consequences of their playfulness—as they are "in the moment" of fun and not thinking about the future—a characteristic they share with both **Elvians** and **Unicorns** at times.

Amethyst Crystal: *(breaking in impatiently)* Well, you know, sometimes people say our Being moves like lightning and talks so fast—I would think that would mean we're of the Fairy Essence. But how could that be—when we have the qualities of an Elvian nature, too? And speaking of the Elvian energy—are we there yet?

Astro: *(poking fun at A.C.'s eagerness)* I don't suppose anyone has ever mentioned to your Being that she's a bit impatient, have they?

Amethyst Crystal: *(with total innocence, as best as it can pretend)* Whatever gave you that idea?

(All the members as well as the Being and Astro laugh out loud, enjoying the joke.)

Light is a kingdom of consciousness,
and it has a purpose in existence.
—Barbara Marciniak, *Bringers of the Dawn*

Make happiness the priority.
Accept your personal authenticity,
the freedom to be yourself.
—Barry Neil Kaufmann, *Happiness Is a Choice*

CHAPTER EIGHT

THE ELVIAN ESSENCE

"If it's not fun, it's best left undone."

—Paul Reps

Astro: You were asking, Amethyst Crystal, about the **Elvian Essence**? So, here we are.

(The Being eagerly pays attention, but with some hesitancy too, thinking to itself how it identifies also with the Fairy and Angelic viewing places, or at least it can remember times when it seemed to express those points of view....)

Astro: *(launching right in)* The **Elvian Essence** is that of the "playful agitator," holding the space among us of fun, laughter, and not-taking-things-quite-so-seriously. For the **Elvians are fun-loving, fun-seeking, adventurous, and *harmless* pranksters.** They like to stir up the pot but innocently disclaim doing the stirring. By *harmless*, we mean that they certainly don't mean to hurt anyone, and if any harm does occur unintentionally as a result of their play, the **Elvian** nature would feel extremely sorry about it. In a perpetual state of wonder, with childlike inquisitiveness, these mischievous delights love to laugh, have fun, and peek and poke at the world in new ways. For the **Elvians'** gift is to ungel the seriousness on planet Earth by bringing Wholeness into the flow, keeping humanity from stagnating.

Physically, the **Elvian Essence** in human form generally appears as a taller thinner version of the **Fairy,** with longer legs and a shorter upper body. They are light and playful, with a BIG dose of mischief, and they pride themselves on not getting caught. Their continuous motion helps them "get away" quickly, and they have a chameleon-like ability to blend into the surrounding background when necessary or whenever it suits their purposes. This *disappear-ability* is necessary, because unlike the **Fairy** and **Angelic,** the **Elvian** is earthbound and has no wings to escape its self-created difficulties. Don't be fooled by the fact that they don't have a set pace, for they can vary their speed; the determining factor is that they're just about *always* in motion, with lots of activities and then even *more* activities, even when they're tired. In fact, Elvians get their energy from staying in motion, and that's also how they stay safe—along with their ability to blend into the background. After all, it's hard to hit a moving target. This "in-motion" vitality makes them natural exercisers, travelers, and minglers.

Although the **Elvian** shares the **Fairy**'s lightness, playfulness, and finely-tuned sensitivity, this energy is naturally more grounded, being earthbound. Unassuming and matter-of-factly inquisitive, they are always ready for new horizons and adventures, liking a great deal of changing scenery and variety, which does not mean they don't enjoy their homes when they are finished wandering about. In pursuing new adventures, the **Elvian Essence** wants to accommodate folks—but only to a point, and only sort of, at that, because its attention span tends to be rather short, since they are likely to already be focused on the next item on their agenda.

Above all, this prankster simply cannot resist "coloring outside the lines," as it were. Just *having* to stir the pot a bit, they're ones to always ask, "Well, *who says* it has to be that way?"—because they will always want to ungel any set-ness. Besides, they have a hard time believing that *anything* on Earth has got to be *that* serious. To an **Elvian** nature, "rules" are great, but they're also a perfect thing to bend and play with, so the **Elvian** tends to want to treat rules more like guidelines instead of blanket applications, and adapt them to the situation. This fireball of energy sometimes seems to go out of its way to look for fun, instigate adventures, and get things done via "other-than-usual" channels, operating not quite within all the "set" boundaries and playing "between the cracks" of the recognized conventions. The **Elvian** hates to hear—but quite often runs into—comments such as, *It's serious!* or, *I can't believe you think this is funny!*

Typically, an **Elvian** will set a practical joke, then deny being involved. Or on the way home from school as a child, they are the ones who always urge the others to take a "detour" or cut through the cemetery on Halloween, or hatch any sort of plot to have some fun along the way. Or, fascinated with the interactions between humans, an **Elvian** may spread information and set things in motion to set up an encounter between two other people, then sit in the background, giggling at what happens. The **Elvian Essence** may also enjoy planning surprises or doing things for others, without necessarily having the others find out who set it all up. Likewise, the **Elvian Essence** has a fascination for shiny, sparkly objects, and they may find themselves "borrowing" them without asking—and later returning them on the sly. **All these actions, again, are** *harmless* **in intent and come from the point of view of reminding humanity not to be quite so serious about third-dimensional reality**—after all, it's not *true* reality, just a game or a *play* we're engaged in.

A person with **Elvian** tendencies can up its amps a bit—for example, to meet someone else's agenda for the moment—but when done, they're *done*—and *out of there!* During any endeavor that involves a sustained level of intensity, you might very well find their eyes glazing over at the point when it takes more energy to be "present" than they are inclined to muster. At that point, they are *hasta luego*, looking for the nearest exit. Sometimes sneaky, sometimes secretive, **Elvians** tend to be nonconfrontive and may also be inclined to bolt if it looks like they're about to get cornered or caught. However, if noticed or focused on, they can hold their own quite nicely, due to their natural talents as manifestors.

Yes, **Elvians** tend to be excellent manifestors because they're out meeting people—in motion, connecting here and there—and as a somewhat natural consequence, things just seem to happen, and no one outcome is innately more important than another. Highly adaptable, they can live in open possibility more easily than some, and therefore manifestation is more of a daily ingredient in their lives.

Hating the ordinary and daily routine, the Elvian Essence seeks the unordinary in every day's scenario. Repetition, routine, and sameness are anathema to this energy, so to combat stagnation they prefer to make *everything* into a game. This quality also helps them talk to just about anyone. A jack-of-all-trades and very good at many things, the **Elvian Essence** moves easily among all groups, adapting its conversation to whomever they're with at the time. Above others, this Essence can *schmooze* with the political liberals in one moment and the ultraconservatives in the next without missing a beat. In fact, Elvians can be great salespeople, because they can blend and adapt to the background so easily. However, this same quality may make it difficult for them to stand up for themselves, and it may cause others to view them as insincere. Also, if they blend in *too* much and get trapped, they run the risk of not just "looking like a tree" but "becoming" one and losing their sense of Self.

The Being: *(pondering its Elf-ness)* So Astro, what happens when this nature is *off-line* or *way-off-line?*

Astro: *(pulled back to the moment)* Oh, I almost forgot—thanks for reminding me. You see, in this case, when **off-line,** this nature reverts back to what is considered "socially correct behavior." And what I mean by that is, they will tend to be model citizens and follow the rules more exactly—but their spark and enthusiasm will be dimmed considerably. This drop in energy might also show up as a tendency to want to "control" the situation or another, as in "not making waves." Also when **off-line,** the **Elvian**'s sense of Self will be highly distorted, as they've adapted to everyone and everything, which can result in nasty behavior at times, vs. simply mischievous. This distortion leads to judgment or a lack of interest in life. And **way-off-line,** bitterness or envy in an **Elvian** may result in minor criminal behavior. **As with any nature, our strength becomes our weakness when we are at-a-tilt or out-of-balance within our Selves.** And the key identifying factor in the **Elvian Essence** is that their constant adaptation to changing environments can then turn into a curse.

(Almost in a panic, Gabriella tugs on Astro's energy field, momentarily halting the Astral Body Therapist's thoughts.)

Gabriella: Excuse me, Astro. I'm so sorry to interrupt, but I have to tell you all—*this* is why I used to be so scared all of the time. I know you all thought it was just because I was weak, and I know I was weak, but that wasn't what was behind it all. Having been "on the road" for over seven years—*can you imagine* the energy it takes to *constantly adapt* to a whole new world, every time we would stop to visit someone?

Unicorn: *(experiencing its own revelation)* Gee, Gabriella, we have shared the Moment of Now with our Being all of these years, and it never dawned on me what all this moving around would do to you. I was always more aware of my own tired-ness.

(Unicorn gives Gabriella another hug.)

Amethyst Crystal: *(not to be left out)* Actually, I can't believe how short-sighted I have been, not to recognize that all these thoughts I throw out to you two are not as easy to do as they are for me to think up. Will you forgive me again, Gabriella, for not recognizing the important role you play in the quality of life that our Being experiences?

Gabriella: *(very moved by Amethyst Crystal's acknowledgment)* Of course, A.C.; I don't mention this to point nonexistent fingers but just to let you all know that I am beginning to see my own contributions, or lack thereof, to life as we know it through our Being. I guess you could say my sense of my own avenue of communication is filling in.

(Gabriella expands its energy field to embrace Unicorn, Amethyst Crystal, the Being, and—not wishing to leave any-one out—Astro, too.)

Astro: *(experiencing a moment of nostalgia)* I have to say that I've missed you body representatives and Being, and I'm so glad you were dreaming of me and allowed me to reenter your energy patterns. But, I have a few more thoughts to share, and

I encourage you to listen intently, so you can see if this **Elvian Essence** fits with what you know of your "Self."

(While viewing all the fluctuations in their energy fields, Astro pauses dramatically before continuing.)

Astro: This dynamic of energy, the **Elvian Essence,** may sometimes appear to be a bit of a con artist, because they can so easily sign you up to their cause out of their belief in their momentary convictions or "role." It's just that the role—and corresponding convictions—might be changed on the next occasion. The **Elvian Essence,** therefore, naturally balks at fitting exactly into a mold or when others try to manipulate or curtail its energy or freedom. *Don't fence me in!* makes a perfect motto for the **Elvian** nature, for their internal viewing space propels them to get people out of their ruts, and if these pranksters feel that they've been put into a box with no way out, they will find six ways from Sunday to escape. The **Elvian Essence,** therefore, finds its destiny in movement—in all different directions—to reclaim its freedom, or just for the sake of *lightly* stirring things up.

(The Being begins to feel a slight uneasiness surfacing, as its awareness catches questioningly on the words, "just for the sake of **lightly** *stirring things up..."?)*

We need fun and laughter to sweep away the depressing thoughts too often found in our world.
—Tanis Heliwell, *Summer with the Leprechauns*

How could I have known that it was to be a place
*of unpredictable **adventure, magic, terror,** and **romance**?*

—Dan Millman, *Way of the Peaceful Warrior*
(emphasis added)

When you discard arrogance, complexity,
and a few other things that get in the way,
sooner or later you will discover that simple,
childlike, and mysterious secret,
known to those of the Uncarved Block:
Life is Fun.

—Benjamin Holt, *The Tao of Pooh*

You've got to AC-CEN-TU-ATE the POSITIVE,
E-LIM-I-NATE the NEGATIVE,
Latch on to the Affirmative,
And don't mess with Mr. In-Between!

—popular mid-20th century song

CHAPTER NINE

THE UNICORN ESSENCE

"When you wish upon a star, your dreams come true."
—*Walt Disney song from* Pinocchio, *sung by Jiminy Cricket*

(Each of the members, lost in its wonder of exactly how much each of the Essences seems to fit the Being they serve, momentarily faze out, from all the input to their sensibilities. Meanwhile, the Being ponders the depth of each Essence described so far, sensing an affinity to each, leaving it in a quandary as to exactly which Essence it is.)

Astro: *(bringing every energy's attention back to the "present" moment)* Now we come to the gentlest, most sensitive of all the Magical Essences—the **Unicorn.** For the **Unicorn** literally lives in a "magical forest" on planet Earth while holding open the awareness on Earth for the **Belief in Wholeness, Magic, Love, Oneness, the perfect orchestration of the universe, and the inherent harmony and value of all things.** The Unicorns also hold the space of **Safety**—for when all is possible and all is perfect, all are safe. Likewise, they hold the space of **Vulnerability,** the trust and openness that is required for the experience of Love to prevail—in a single word, **Belief.**

Like the mythical unicorn in fairy tales, which can never be "approached" or "caught" but may choose to show itself and allow the touch of someone who is pure of heart, the **Unicorn Essence** exudes a purity that may only be visible to those who are pure themselves.

Ironically, while holding the space for Belief in Wholeness, the **Unicorn** may not feel all that connected to people and in fact may be feeling the most dis-connected to humanity, for very much of the planet is consumed by disbelief in magic and wholeness. Sometimes it even seems as though there are not many **Unicorns** left here on the planet, and in fact, the discord and out-of-whackness has sent most **Unicorns** into hiding, making them the least visible and the most invisible Essence.

The fact is, **Unicorns** aren't often "gotten" and often don't "come out" where they are visible, because people have held this ultimate kind of Belief as something separate from themselves, placing credence instead in separation from their wholeness. Nonetheless, even though people don't "see" **Unicorns**—*i.e.*, don't tend to believe in them—they are definitely *here* among us!

Physical Body Representative (Unicorn):   Hey, Astro, why can't we be this Unicorn Essence? I really like the idea—so who says we have to stay an Elvian energy? I mean, can't people change Essences?

Astro: *(always presenting many viewpoints)* Whoever said you were an **Elvian** nature?

   (Surprised, all awarenesses turn questioningly toward Astro.)

Astro: *(continuing as though on a Sunday stroll through a park)* I mean, you sound as though these are separate entities, or forms—like a suit of clothing to put on. And if you body reps, and you, Being, are viewing this conversation about the invisible realms as if the Essences were separate "things," what do you think other human Beings will do? You see, these Essences are from the beginning of time, which is why, if you believe in many lifetimes, you will have similar issues show up over and over again. However, your individual expression will continue to grow and change within that Essence or viewing space, as there are no limits to the amount of growth possible.

Astro: *(keeping in mind Unicorn's earlier question)* Still, we are only on the fourth pure Essence, which we have called "**Unicorn**." Who knows, Unicorn, maybe your Being's Essence hasn't even been discussed yet.

Amethyst Crystal: *(following the direction of this thinking)* Are you *playing with us,* Astro? I mean, I know we have shown up as this Elvian Essence for most of our Being's life, and I just assumed that was our viewing space.

Astro: *(with a big grin)* A.C., you are such a delight! But to answer your question, I'm not trying to *do* anything—just be in a space of inquiry and possibility. Do you understand me now?

Amethyst Crystal: I get it. You just leave open the doorway to new or different notions, to promote learning, right?

Astro: My point exactly. But to continue about the **Unicorn**... *(regaining its thoughts about the Unicorn Essence)* Many **Unicorns** have experienced lifelong feelings of "not fitting in" or of not being able to fully connect to the things and doings of this Earth realm. When they're down, they retreat into invisibility and may not be "heard from" for some time. On the other hand, when feeling their oats, their strong belief and support can part the Red Seas—and this is in line with the **Wizard** energy.

(The Being feels a disquieting and involuntary inner discomfort, almost a jolt, every time it hears Astro mention the Wizard Essence.)

Astro: *(continuing without a pause)* So how can you locate a **Unicorn**? It's in their enthusiasm or passion for their **niche**. Their safe "niche" might be their computer activities, home, job, office, garden, art work, favorite cause, or children. **When Unicorns are in their particular niche, they exude feelings of security, confidence, connectedness, and all-out support**—so strongly so that they can be mistaken for a **Dwarvian** or **Wizard** Essence. However, this energy does not translate to activities or arenas where that safety is not absolute, in which case they may appear diabolically opposite to the confidence they exude when in their niche—to the point where you might think they're not feeling well or that they've become an entirely different person. They may appear to be solitary creatures or workaholics at times, always in their shop or workplace, or never around groups or seeking out social situations—unless sociability is their "niche." Or, when they are out of their element, they may appear less than their vibrant Self, or have nothing to say. For in many cases the **Unicorn** would rather remain hidden in its magical forest than be "out there" and exposed, having to counter the disbelief and discord in the world. **From time to time, it's almost essential that Unicorns seek out solitude or pull off the track for a while, often in Nature, for indeed this is their rejuvenation period,** so that they can come back out into the world, ready to participate. This aspect of the **Unicorn** relates to the close friendship between **Unicorn** and **Elvian** Essences. Because the **Elvian** has the ability to direct life traffic, it can provide the **Unicorn** the protection it needs when out and about in Life.

You see, **Unicorns** are designed to "re-member wholeness" and hold the space of this Belief for everyone, while in manifested form, wherever they are on the planet, at all times. **It is their *profound knowingness* that this world is designed to be a magical place in which everyone has the safety to fully self-express, and that is the crux of their existence.** And they know that this quality is found in Nature as well, so these people tend to like to hike and be outdoors in the mountains and the forest. Not surprisingly, few people operate from such deep belief at this time on the planet, and it is this very deep belief that often brings the **Unicorn** to a state of depression when faced with too many discombobulating judgmental life experiences.

Gabriella: Astro, are you referring to the *off-line* status for the Unicorn Essence?

Astro: Gosh, thanks, Gabriella. I really wasn't thinking one way or another, but this is indeed *off-line* for the **Unicorn.** I might even go so far as to say that being "down in the dumps" is a very real concern for the gentle **Unicorn** nature, at least for as long as the planet continues to waver in its perceptual view. Another *off-line* trait shows up when the **Unicorns'** strength becomes their weakness, and they choose rarely to leave their niche, for any reason. Taken to an extreme, *way-off-line* **Unicorns** may appear nonresponsive to conversations, activities, and interactions in the world. This "shutting down" to Life is their response to a world seemingly bent on separation.

(Simply because the Being's physical body representative happens to be seen as a Unicorn, all other eyes turn to it

involuntarily, as they imagine the depth of difficulty for any Essence as beautiful as the animal before them.)

Astro: *(also noting the purity of the physical body representative's radiance)* In fact, some **Unicorns** may appear to others to be "living in a fantasy world," as if they are hiding from "reality." If they tend to be self-deluding in this third-dimensional realm, it is because they really *do* live in another world—*true reality*—which holds the space of Universal Truth for all humanity.

Exuding innocence and purity, **Unicorns** wander the planet as if they are always in the Magical Forest, unaware that the bullets are flying around them. Unfortunately, if they get hit, and many do, they sometimes lose all hope, for indeed, they have no protection from negativity and confinement. When the **Unicorn** has been curtailed, disbelieved, discounted, or shorted, it will tend to disappear or withdraw, and its highly sensitive, deeply feeling nature takes such experiences so much to heart that the **Unicorn** becomes very fearful and vulnerable, to the point of depression, as they just cannot *imagine* that the planet can exhibit such lack of support!

What's surprising about the sensitive **Unicorn** nature is that they can be quite stubborn at times, digging in their hooves when someone tries to pry them from their niche when they're not feeling inclined to come out. And if pushed or backed into a corner by themselves or others, they can exhibit quite an explosive temper.

Gabriella: *(popping in with fervor)* Boy, I can understand that point of view! I mean, just from my emotional standpoint, sometimes I can feel so full of energy that it's as if I'm about to burst like a volcano.

(turning toward Amethyst Crystal) And that's what you used to call my "lack of control." *Now* I can understand why you were trying so hard to bring that part of me back into balance.

Amethyst Crystal: *(looking over to Gabriella and enjoying the feeling of being honored by its colleague)* Why, thank you, Gabriella.

Astro: *(smiling appreciatively at A.C. and Gabriella's exchange)* You see, the **Unicorn**'s reluctance to come out in the world makes sense when you realize how much buildup occurs in their Being's emotional body. For whenever they mix worlds—mix metaphors, as it were—they can get tripped up, and then they tend to get hurt. Plainly stated, they lose their magic if they lose contact with their Magical Forest—*i.e.,* their safety, their niche—and if they lose Belief in themselves, they become just a plain "horse."

They can even desire death over life when the natural flow of support seems low or nonexistent—or they simply remain at the effect of consequences and circumstances throughout life, never fully regaining their gift of exquisite sensitivity and belief in true reality.

(The physical body representative, Unicorn, lets out a deep, heart-wrenching sigh, and all invisible eyes turn toward it and wait. Finally, with tears in its eyes, Unicorn shares its concern.)

Unicorn: *(with a wavering voice)* I know you said, Astro, that all viewing places are within all consciousness—however, I feel so deeply connected to this Unicorn Essence. Am I just getting too involved with what you are saying? I'm confused.

Astro: *(feeling the heartfelt connection with Unicorn)* Aren't we all! As I said before, your Being brought *you* forth as in image for her physical body representative, because of the sensitivity in her physical form. So it's not surprising that you feel this Essence so deeply at times, even though at other times you may be very gregarious and boisterous.

Unicorn: *(feeling a flood of safety and gratitude)* You know what I appreciate most about you, Astro? You "get" me, and at the same time, you don't attempt to "fix" me or alter me, or make me have to be one way. And so I am free to relax, even though at the moment I haven't a clue where this is leading.

Astro: *(almost blushing)* Wow, Unicorn, that's about the nicest thing anyone has said of me, to me! *(And with a look of love in Unicorn's direction, Astro continues...)*

On the other hand, a **Unicorn** who is supported and safe in its view of the world can provide the *ultimate* support to others, equating giving with living, much like the **Angelics.** Because the **Unicorn** believes in all possibility, it holds value in all things, naturally holding everyone as full power, full magnificence, and so on. So **just the touch of a Unicorn's hand or "presence" can provide another with the connection to All, which shows up as peace, contentment, safety, and "being at ease"—otherwise known as** *Love.*

Amethyst Crystal: *(stifling a hint of a yawn)* This airy-fairy, lovey-dovey notion is wonderful, Astro, but are there any concrete physical attributes we can look for?

Astro: *(chuckling)* Oh, A.C., I so appreciate you bringing us back to the topic at hand. Okay, so, physically speaking, **Unicorns** may be on the tall side, lanky and substantial in appearance. But more than mere size, the **Unicorn Essence** makes for a *substantial person*—with an immense inner dimension. Interior-knowers, the **Unicorns** appear to hold the space of "within," and this internal substance emanates as a heartfelt *presence*, even though they too have mentally and emotionally-based means of communicating.

Unicorns are naturally drawn to all animals, and they may seem horse-like in energy—strong and courageous at moments, skittish at others. If the **Unicorn** is not getting enough nurturing from other humans or life situations, they will seek out the animal kingdom for hugs, companionship, and unconditional Love. Being in tune with Nature and Magic, **Unicorns** are the most likely Essence to be "animal conscious." In fact, this tendency can lead to being *off-line* for the **Unicorn,** up to *way-off-line*, depending on their life circumstances, when they truly start to prefer the animal world over the human. One day I ran across a bumper sticker that pretty well indicates this sentiment: *The more humans I meet, the better I like my dog.*

For the **Unicorn,** out-of-whackness leads to protecting itself, whereby it can deflect brashness; however, **kindness will always get through to the Unicorn.** The difficulty for the **Unicorn** crops up when someone gains its trust and then subsequently shorts it or pulls the rug out from under it, leaving the **Unicorn** devastated and retreating to its magical niche—not to be seen again for many moons.

(Again, looking at the physical body representative and seeing a Unicorn, the Being revels in the magnitude of what the physical body enables it, as consciousness, to do.)

Astro: *(grinning inwardly at the Being's awareness)* As far as being "grounded," **Unicorns** can appear grounded in their niche, but since they "live" in a magical reality, they can appear equally "ungrounded" at times. Also, they have the magical ability to "fly," by virtue of their magical horn, and this ability is one of the reasons why the **Elvian** energy, in particular, likes to pair up with a **Unicorn**. Like the **Elvian** nature, the **Unicorn** balks at being backed into a corner, labeled in a box-like category, caged, or surprised from behind, and it needs to be free to maneuver, to appear and disappear at will.

The **Unicorn** is *yin* and *yang*—both substantial and insubstantial, sunlight and shadow. *There* and *not there*. Feeling safe—except when they're not. Exuding support—except when they've lost belief. Appearing strong—except when they're under attack and cut off from support and safety. Again, they may be highly visible, when in their niche and feeling safe—or they may be completely invisible.

The **Unicorn** is even more sensitive than the **Fairy**—and extremely nonconfrontive—unless provoked, as *safety* is so important to it. Like the **Fairy** Essence, **Unicorns** may appear very light and nonassuming, but this lightness is overshadowed in the **Unicorns** by the substance and depth of their convictions and beliefs, which are clearly seen in their expressions of great devotion and generosity. Because of their natural, generous nature, **Unicorns** can easily be drawn into other people's projects or agendas at the expense of their own interests, so it's important for them to emerge from their niches of their own accord. That is to say—if they feel like joining in, great; if not—back off.

The depth of the **Unicorn**'s convictions is also why they can be so very convincing and charismatic when giving out a message in which their certainty or knowingness is evident. Their naturally high belief and confidence can motivate them to amazing feats, but again, when they've run into the disconnectedness and when uncertain about safety, they can immediately seem very shy, nervous, and meek. They may toe-dabble at new endeavors until they feel safe or make several fly-by's before succeeding in connecting with or entering a new realm of activity or experience. This tentativeness in some situations is one way to tell them apart from the **Angelic** Essence, as **Angelics** operate from a full base of knowingness and power, no matter their surroundings.

It almost goes without saying that it's very important that the **Unicorn** be able to get together with like-mindedness. For example, **Fairy** folks can cheer it up, bring out its playfulness, and "polish up its magical horn." **Angelics** and other **Unicorns** can provide mutually-giving, heartfelt support. The **Elvian** energy protects and prods the **Unicorn** out of its stupor, if need be, and readily adopts the **Unicorn** as a "best friend" for adventuring. Also, a balanced **Wizard** understands and gains comfort from the **Unicorn**'s gentle presence. Bottom line, **Unicorns** thrive on magic, encouragement, and the ability to go into invisible retreat at times.

(As Astro pauses to reorganize its thoughts, Unicorn, the physical body representative, ponders the deep connection it feels to this Unicorn Essence, as if it must be more than a coincidence that it, its Self, came forth as a Unicorn image ... and then it wonders, But how can that be?)

It is only with the heart that one can see rightly;
What is essential is invisible to the eye.
—Antoine de St.-Exupéry, *The Little Prince*

I could never leave my forest: I know how to live here,
I know how everything smells and tastes and is.
What could I ever search for in this world, except this again?

—Peter S. Beagle, *The Last Unicorn*

Magic has to be believed—that's the only way it's real.

—Frances Hodgson Burnett, *A Little Princess*

In order to take control of our lives and accomplish something of
lasting value, sooner or later we need to learn to Believe....
We simply need to believe in the power that's within us, and use it.
When we do that, and stop imitating others and competing
against them, things begin to work for us.

—Benjamin Holt, *The Tao of Pooh*

CHAPTER TEN

THE DWARVIAN ESSENCE

"A true friend is one who sifts through all our joys and woes,
and keeps only what is of value."

(As Astro continues to share the "pure" traits of the six Magical Essences, the Being, Amethyst Crystal, Unicorn, and Gabriella, each in their own thoughts, find themselves humbled by the hugeness of this Essence awareness.)

Astro: *(noting the awe before plunging into the most earthbound of the six pure Essences)* Most fittingly, since humans do live their lives in a third-dimensional Earth-plane reality, **the Dwarvian Essence grounds the cosmic forces into the Earth.** After all, it's rather a good thing, don't you think, that at least one of the Essences fully holds the space of grounded-ness—for otherwise, humanity might literally "fly off the planet" from lack of gravity. *(Astro laughs at its own cosmic joke.)* By grounding natural energy into day-to-day Earth activities, **Dwarvians** consistently seek to initiate energy into a humanly workable fashion. And the **Dwarvian Essence** really can "do" planet Earth—while to them, it may seem as though the rest of humanity tends to make it up as they go along, and haphazardly, at that.

Not surprisingly, the **Dwarvian Essence** is knowable through such qualities as **dependability, accountability,**

steadfastness, and **consistency,** and if you are a friend of theirs, you are a friend for life. The **Dwarvians** emanate security and certainty from a practical, Earthbound point of view, as opposed to the **Angelics,** who emanate security and certainty from their unshakable knowing of connectedness to Totality.

(Totally off the subject, Amethyst Crystal and Unicorn involuntarily let out a quiet snicker at the notion of how a dwarf looks in fairy tales.)

Astro: *(having picked up their inner thoughts)* You have to cast aside your programmed images that dwarves are short and squatty, with large noses. It would be more appropriate to recall the perfect forms of the gods and goddesses of mythology, because on the physical side, the **Dwarvian** energy shows up as good-looking humans. Whether male or female, exercised or not, this handsomeness or beauty is often a given.

Emanating a sense of solid beauty, the **Dwarvian Essence** is the most likely to be perfectly proportioned in form, such as having as much body height above the waist as below, in a somewhat solid presentation. The so-called "perfect male" and "perfect female" figures are products of the **Dwarvian** patterning, as opposed to the **Fairy** folk, who have to "live with" always looking younger than their years. However, the **Dwarvian** bodies may not be as flexible as others, which often reflects their approach to life, making it like pulling teeth to get them to change direction, at times.

The **Dwarvians** are probably the *most helpful* of the Essences, largely because knowing how to maneuver on this planet is a given for them. In fact, throughout Earth history, we have seen this Essence in motion as bending over backward in order to see that the third-dimensional items are handled. The **knight in shining armor,** the **hero or heroine to the rescue,** the **model citizen** with a **heart of gold,** and the **"salt of the earth"** are all apt images for the **Dwarvians.**

The Dwarvian viewing space on Totality is methodical, practical, down-to-earth, loyal, and devoted. The **Dwarvian** nature is also confident, because they "know how to do things" on Earth, and if they don't know, they will persevere to find out. They may even tend to dominate others, due to their organizational insights. They naturally want to support others but must also watch out not to virtually "roll over" others with their persistent, highly matter-of-fact, and confident points of view. If off-balanced or *off-line*, the **Dwarvian Essence** may tend to curtail, discount, and control others.

Extremely stubborn and rather slow to change, a **Dwarvian** nature will "head on into the fray" or into new challenges and tenaciously stick to its point of view, unafraid of confrontation. Sometimes the **Dwarvian** will stay around longer in a project or relationship than serves them, when it may in fact be timely to move on. The **Dwarvians** share confrontational abilities with the **Angelics,** who confront more gently, for wholeness—as well as the **Wizards,** whose vision and drive to stir up and transmute everything make them naturally confrontive.

Ideal employees, **on-line Dwarvians** will consistently carry out their work, keeping a steady, hardy pace and routine that rarely varies, even under pressure. It is possible for them to speed up if necessary for a short sprint, but then they will return rather quickly to their customary pace and routine. Their tenacity also helps them "keep going no matter what."

Because of their helpfulness, **Dwarvians** tend to be wonderful friends. They may develop friendships slowly, however, and those that they do hold are apt to be "good for life." Also, if you look around for the **Dwarvians** in your life, you will find them often helping the downtrodden.

It may not surprise you that **Fairies** are often paired up with **Dwarvians,** for the **Fairies,** being the *least* grounded, are less inclined to want to handle all the little "details" of third-dimensional living, while **Dwarvians,** on the other hand, being the *most* grounded, are naturally oriented towards helpfully handling the details and easily adapting to the world. However, the earthbound **Dwarvian** must watch out not to overrun the **Fairy** unintentionally through its solid, consistent point of view, or expect the **Fairy** to become like itself and get "grounded," which, as we discussed before, can literally sever the wings and drain the life force out of the **Fairy** nature.

Just because **Dwarvians** are grounded, however, does not mean they aren't spiritually-inclined. Unlike the **Fairy** folk, who reach Totality through going way out into the starry heavens, **Dwarvians** seek Totality or Wholeness through going deep within themselves, or deep into Nature, as reflected through the rituals of Native peoples all over Earth. Shamanic traditions, animal totems, and crystal, herbal, and stone medicine all evolved from the **Dwarvian Essence.** The **Dwarvians** are the "Keepers of the Earth," and from their point of view from Earth-groundedness, the starry heavens and cosmos appear *huge.* For, **if one closes one's eyes and looks far enough inward—one finds one's spiritual Self as far out into the cosmos as if one had headed that way in the first place. This is the heart of the Dwarvian nature—**

going "within" to reach wholeness. And whether you get there from going way off into the cosmos, like the **Fairy Essence,** or deep within the Self, like the **Dwarvian,** both directions take you to the same place, as all roads lead to Home.

Unfortunately, a **Dwarvian Essence** who is *out-of-whack* or off-kilter in its connection to Self may seek to hold others back from unfoldment or pull them down. And the one being pulled "down to earth" may feel as though they're being *driven* into the ground, not just placed onto it. When *off-line,* the **Dwarvian**'s steadiness becomes plodding and dense, emanating a stubborn heaviness, especially when they feel negative or unhappy. The same as for any Essence, their strength becomes their weakness when they are viewing life from a place of separation and judgment.

It is a Universal Truth that when one feels separate from the whole—or family, or job—one's greatest lessons come through loss or tragedy, but when one reconnects with the Self, others, and the world or Totality, one's lessons are encountered through gain and mutual support. This truth is very knowable to the **Dwarvian Essence** and a motivation for its seeking to help others experience their value and worth—so that all can experience this cooperative way of living.

A Dwarvian who is estranged from its spiritual depths may be ultra-concrete and disbelieving of anything that can't be perceived with the five physical senses: *If I can't see it, it's not true.* Thus, an *off-line* or *way-off-line* **Dwarvian** may exhibit no belief at all in the magical realms and may pooh-pooh entirely the invisible aspects of Totality, if it has no experiential awareness of it.

The **Dwarvians** can become so earth-bound, if out of balance, that they end up in a rut, not seeming to be able to get into action to change, or seeming to be the world's best procrastinators. If *way-off-line,* they may be so set in their actions that they pull other folks down with them simply by holding too tightly to "what has been" vs. opening up to "what the possibilities might be"—giving no one room to grow, change, unfold, or evolve, including themselves.

(Astro pauses for effect.)

Gabriella: *(pondering these last thoughts)* Astro, regarding what you have said about the Dwarvian propensity to stay in the "status quo," do you think this has added to the less-than-supportive image that has been given to dwarves in some fairy tales?

Astro: *(full of glee)* Quite right, Gabriella—but perhaps the less flamboyant form is actually more of a short-sightedness on humanity's part of the value of steadfastness and consistency during change. And now, it's possible that human Beings are finally beginning to grasp the value of all perceiving points, for like the threads in a tapestry, when all are present, the tapestry becomes that much more brilliant.

(Gabriella, Unicorn, and Amethyst Crystal, feeling much better about these Essences in general, as they get to know each one, are glad nonetheless that there is only one more to consider. Meanwhile, the Being remains silent and watchful.)

I was always looking outside myself for strength and confidence, but it comes from within. It is there all the time.

—Anna Freud

I have come with living waters,
these healing ways of the Wolves,
the living waters, the spirit crystal,
ha wo ho.

—Lebi'd, a Kwakiutl shaman,
on his return from the land of the Dead

But I know every rock and tree and creature
Has a life, has a spirit, has a name.

—Stephen Schwartz, "Colors of the Wind,"
from Disney's *Pocahontas*

Deep in their roots, all flowers keep the light...

—Theodore Roethke

Speak to the earth,
and it shall teach thee.

—Job 12:8

♡ CHAPTER ELEVEN ♡

THE WIZARD ESSENCE

"Whether for benefit or ill, the Red Seas WILL be parted..."

Astro: *(with a mischievous twinkle in its eye, having noted the body members' thoughts of fatigue and the Being's wariness)* And now, we come to the final Essence to describe in terms of its "pure" traits. At the beginning of creation, it seems the Universe intuited a space that would come into form and contain **a full expression of each of the other five energies, as well as a highly dynamic, manifestive intensity**—and the name for this Essence is *Wizard.*

(Amethyst Crystal, Unicorn, and Gabriella, all feeling as if they've been hit by a brick, silently surmise the implications of this statement.)

(Astro, noting the reaction, continues to pause, waiting for a verbal reaction from any one of them. With none forthcoming, Astro continues.)

Astro: For, the **Wizard Essence** can appear in any form, as any Essence, at any time—and can literally shape-shift itself instantly from moment to moment. These are your **Alchemists**, and from lifetime to lifetime, they will choose a physical form, from among all the other Essences, that they feel will best suit them in their next life. In other words, they can adapt themselves to a voluptuous **Angelic** form, a very litheful **Fairy** presentation, a tall energetic **Elvian** form, a sturdy **Dwarvian** body, or a substantial yet gentle **Unicorn** presence. In addition, the physical form most associated with the **Wizard** Essence, if it chooses to show up as a **Wizard** in any given lifetime—is **next to *no form* at all.**

The alchemical aspect of the Wizard almost forces these folks to relentlessly work with *transformation* and *manifestation*. Otherwise stated—for better or for worse, they *will* manifest. And it's this intense overwhelming drive that drives every other Essence to the brink of losing their cookies!

(Having tried to brighten the news, Astro looks over to find that the members are now showing strong looks of despair at the suspicion that their Being might have arrived at its Essence. In addition, the Being itself wears a look of shock and horror, along with one of full recognition that indeed it without a doubt has arrived at its Essence—given the fact that it could identify 100% with every Essence thus far described. Yet, the Being feels deeply distressed by the implication that this nature can overwhelm the other Essences—even while Amethyst Crystal's memory banks speedily confirm that yes, this "overwhelm" dynamic has in fact often surfaced in the Being's relationships and activities in life.)

Astro: *(continuing, despite the fact that the Being and its members are still disoriented in their shock at this revelation—knowing that the only way through this news is to deliver all of it)* You see, perhaps the **Wizard**'s most distinguishing characteristic is that **it appears different in different settings and at different times.** This *strength* is what gives the **Wizard Essence** its greatest contribution to the whole, for indeed, no other Essence can truly see the many different viewing points and varied positions, plus the *value* of each, in the way that this nature can. It can transform from **Angelic** connectedness, into **Elvian** mischief, into vulnerable **Unicorn** sensitivity, upon a moment's notice. True, the **Elvian** can also manifest quickly, but **the Wizard's distinguishing characteristic will be the continuous intensity of its manifestation.**

(While Astro speaks, the Being's three dense-body representatives also ponder and feel more fully their deep identification with each of the Essences, as Astro has described them, and they all begin to "get" with a deep certainty that the "Wizard" nature is truly knowable to them.)

Astro: *(continuing to press ahead rapidly)* **It is in the Wizard's nature to "get" humanity from all points of view and to integrate diverse perceptual viewing places.** In their strongest, most balanced and *on-line* expressions, *no one* supports all the Essences as fully as the Wizard. And in its *on-line* presentation, **the best of all Essences, including its own, resides in the Wizard.**

(The Being starts to come out of its shock, as it suddenly begins to feel a sense of its contribution to humanity, but before it can speak, Amethyst Crystal jumps in.)

Amethyst Crystal: Okay, Astro. Am I seeing this clearly? Are you telling us that our Being is this Wizard Essence?

Astro: *(as cool as a cucumber)* You tell me.

Amethyst Crystal: Well, at first I was deathly afraid it was true. But as you kept talking, I began to think that maybe being a Wizard is not such a bad thing. I have to admit that I have seen these Wizard attributes come through my conversation at times— when I have literally "run over" another, simply because I was speaking a thought to myself out loud. I don't even have to look far in my memory banks for a phrase that I use very often, which is, *I'm always chewing on my foot, for having stuck it halfway down my throat—and apologizing profusely for some inappropriate behavior.*

Gabriella: *(getting with the awareness)* And I'm realizing that I really do have a lot of enthusiasm at times—so much that I can frequently enroll people in our Being's programs, by sheer will.

Unicorn: *(not to be left out, jumping in practically before Gabriella finishes speaking)* And you know, a lot of people tell me how *thin* I am—while in fact I eat like a horse.

(Knowing that all of its members are talking about its Self, the Being, feeling quite exposed, readies its Self to respond to this new information. Sensing that their Being is about to speak, the members turn three sets of respectful non-eyes toward their Being and silently wait for the Being to compose its Self.)

The Being: *(in a very vulnerable space, close to tears)* You know, all these years, I always thought I was just *different*—that somehow maybe God/Universe made an error in my case. I seemed always to talk too loud, too fast, or just not "get" the social graces of human life. And yet I was always so moved by people's *magnificence* that I tended to *flood* their domain rather than just embrace it, sometimes causing them to back away from me. And now, *you're telling me that this is my true nature?* Excuse me—but it's taking me a moment to swallow this pill.

Astro: *(compassionately)* While in a human skin-suit, the world appears a much smaller place than it truly is, for a person sees only a small portion of it in any given moment. In your case, you judged this appearance of limitation as Being "out-of-place"—when in truth, your *on-line-ness* was doing its natural job of disrupting stagnant points-of-view, fearful positions, and simple lack of love and support! In truth, you too have had your unfoldments and *off-line* periods. However, somehow you managed to re-member your wholeness in your process of aiding others to re-member it in theirs. **The aloneness you have felt from time to time has stemmed chiefly from your search for colleagues who function at the same level of intensity, the same level of participation, in their own domains.**

And if there's anything, Being, that has unnerved you, it has been to encounter numbers of human Beings who are operating at the under-the-fifty-percent-level in their personal growth. For in this place, you instantly recognize that they are in a downward spiral and heading out of life. And your response is to "gear up" even more when in their presence—seeming to compound your own intensity, as well as the overwhelm experienced by others. It's been kind of a Catch-22 for you—but in case you haven't already noticed, things *are* changing.

(Astro looks over and sees a dawning of recognition in the Being's energy field, and noting that the Being has gotten over its initial shock, proceeds to explain the Wizard Essence more fully.)

Astro: *(delighted at the Being's shift in energy)* **The hallmark of the pure Wizard is intensity: as if driven, its nature is to agitate the status quo and activate energy in a powerful way.** Like the Angelics, Wizards spread around a full base of energy, and they absolutely have a lot to do and a lot to share in life. But whereas the **Angelics** are intensely powerful when they are focused on things, and the **Unicorns** emanate power when they are in their "niche," **Wizards are always intense, and always needing to manifest, manifest, manifest.** Now when they are *on-line,* the **Wizard** can manifest many positive and wonderful things, but when they are *off-line,* the **Wizard** manifests simply horrible things—for example, running over another's conversation and negating their point of view, thus appearing to reduce the other's value. Also, because **Wizards** can see ahead of the situation and operate with such intensity, the speed at which they function can easily overwhelm some of the other Essences, if those others are even slightly off-balance in their own sense of Self or power. Another reason for the overwhelm is that **Wizards** tend to saturate others with energy, motion, ideas, plans, events, and endless possibilities—which is disruptive in its own right to many. An **Elvian** energy might be interested in the short jaunt, but over the long haul, the **Wizard** literally doesn't know when to quit!

Amethyst Crystal: *(identifying with the thoughts)* Oh, do I know what you mean! Like the phrase I'm always saying—that we're one continuous "run-on sentence." Is that what you mean, Astro?

Astro: *(chuckling out loud)* That's definitely saying it, A.C., in light of your own dynamics.

Gabriella: *(a little sheepishly)* Astro, is there a way to let people know that we don't mean to harm them?

Astro: Yes, Gabriella—and here's where your shape-shifting qualities become an asset. For indeed, if you approach another from *their* energy-perceiving place, you become most "get-able" and received. It's only when you stay strictly in that intense **Wizard** mode that you overwhelm or override others.

(Astro, realizing how stirred up the Being has become at this revelation, decides to forge ahead and give as many of the Wizard attributes as possible, to give the Being and its members a chance just to hear and absorb the data.)

Astro: *(plunging in)* Perhaps the best way to approach this is to give you as many facets of your nature as possible, so you can more easily grasp the magnitude of your Essence.

(Despite their initial shock, the Being and its members turn toward Astro, eager to hear more about "their" Essence.)

Astro: *(after clearing its nonexistent throat)* First of all, **Wizards** are knowable as being **impatient to the max,** whereas **Dwarvians** are very patient and **Angelics** also, and an **Elvian**'s eagerness to move about would lean to the fidgety side. The **Wizard**'s impatience is tied to its fascination with *all* experiences, *all* points of view, and the *diversity* of all experiences—and **Wizards** often appear as though they just **cannot "eat up" life fast enough. To the Wizards, nothing and everything is sacred, no possibility is out of the question, and every direction or facet is "get-able."** One company-president Wizard hit the nail on the head when commenting that others found it like "drinking from a fireplug" to be around him.

And whereas the **Unicorn** lives in "all possibility" from an introspective angle, the **Wizard** lives in "all possibility" from an outer-directed dynamic. This outer-directedness sometimes causes the **Wizard,** just in its enthusiasm, to "run over" others, without necessarily intending to—but not necessarily stopping to notice, either. In fact, the **Wizard**'s energy can be rather like a bulldozer, in conversation often running right over another's contribution. Their energy may easily fill the room and dominate it. And if a **Wizard** gets annoyed, it can expand its energy forcefully and rapidly to fill the entire space—and you can just imagine the folks in the immediate vicinity running for cover. However, this does not mean they are invulnerable, for if a **Wizard** has adopted the whole demeanor of another Essence, and another **Wizard** comes at it from a position of wizardry, that force could be demolishing. At the same time, if a **Wizard** were to approach another **Wizard,** and both are currently in their **Wizard** mode, a battle would be underway, for neither one would back down from their position. It's no wonder some Essences feel "on edge" around these movers and shakers.

Amethyst Crystal: *(recognizing the truth still more fully)* Gosh, I've got a million one-liners, which must stem from this Wizard nature, for I'm always saying things like, *You think I've got a lot of energy,*—that is, speaking for our Being—*but just imagine—I have to live with myself all the time.*

(This spot of humor lightens the Being's spirit, and Astro can see that even Unicorn and Gabriella are feeling more playful.)

Astro: *(pressing ahead)* When **on-line,** a **Wizard** will "adopt" the Essence of whomever they are with, because that Essence *is* them as well, and they show up as playful, joyful, and energetic. The **Wizard** can move fast like the **Elvian,** and simply *be* with the **Unicorn,** and wing it with the **Fairy.** In fact, it can move with and through all the Essences. This ability can provide a **Wizard,** if the **Wizard** is in balance, with immense charisma, for it can truly "speak to" and "be with" each human and understand its point of view. Only

when the **Wizard** is *off-line* within itself do the consequences become disastrous, for then the **Wizard**'s intense
drive can turn mean and vicious. *Very-off-line,* this can have
definite criminal implications.

*(Both Gabriella and Unicorn turn toward each other as their
newfound glee starts to fade at this sobering idea.)*

Astro: *(having picked up this quiver)* Not to worry, though. For
remember, **it is the main ingredient of the Wizard Essence
to stir things up and to promote change**—keeping in mind
that in the process you stir yourself up as well. But at the same
time, that's one of the reasons that it is hard to pinpoint a
Wizard Essence—because they have so many diverse ways
of functioning, within as well as without. There simply is no
routine for the **Wizards**—not in their eating, their activity,
their relationships, and certainly not in their jobs—which
makes it very difficult to get any semblance of consistency of
what a **Wizard** actually is. And if you ask them, you'll get a
different answer every time. Added to this, in any given
lifetime, a **Wizard Essence** may show up the entire time as
just one or two parts of its nature—which is an *off-line* way
of functioning, since it's not "Being" its full Self—and then
not understand why some people don't like it! It's no wonder
you didn't "get" your-Self, Being.

*(The Being, trying to digest so much information, is grateful
for Astro's encouragement.)*

Astro: *(reinforcing this direction of speaking)* You see, due to life
circumstances, when a **Wizard** energy does lean to just *one*
part of its nature, many times it's because they are in a
"survival" circumstance, and they lean toward the presentation that they feel best protects them. But at some point, a

Wizard, to be fully on-line, does have to face itself in its full power. In your case, Being, your focus on the **Elvian** chunk of your Self served you in your earlier years, or so you thought. And it's only now that you are able to realize the full spectrum of your Self-expression.

And don't feel bad for not "getting" your Self in your full intensity before now, for since the **Wizard** is so hard to pin down, it will appear the most different, to different people. Just think, suppose someone first meets a **Wizard** who is having a gentle **Unicorn** moment. Imagine their surprise the next time the two meet, and the unsuspecting party suddenly feels as though they're in the presence of a completely different person. For this reason, the best clue to **Wizards** is that their **power** or **intensity** is usually very evident. In other words, even the key traits of the other Essences will come through with an added boost, due to this intense Wizard element. Also, because some **Wizards** lean more toward one or more parts of their nature than others, they may not appear genuine to others—or may get judged for misrepresentation, once their fuller spectrum emerges.

(Astro, looks directly at the Being, sensing it is okay to stop for just a moment to let the gist of this Essence filter in....)

Astro: *(remembering a key point)* And the **Wizard** can get *extremely* focused. They *know how* to operate in this realm, as they have the tools from each Essence at their fingertips. It is true, though, that knowing how to operate on the Earth plane and actually accomplishing it, is a trick for anyone. And yet, the **Wizards'** alchemical, transmuting, shape-shifting abilities help them keep one step ahead of those who would try to "hit" them with negativity, for they can shield, step aside, or transform the force of energy directed towards them, at will—that is, if not caught off-guard while they are in another Essence-mode. And the **Wizards** also have the ability to scan people psychically, whether the **Wizard** is consciously aware of this tactic or not, uncannily homing in on the jugular, and, if tired or distraught, appearing to attack others outright at their weak points.

(Astro, knowing what courage and sincerity it takes for this Being to own up to its nature, pauses to note the current reactions of the Being and its members.)

Gabriella: *(grasping to comprehend—and feeling remorse)* Is it just me, Astro, or does it seem that this Essence is more disconcerting than the rest?

Astro: *(compassionately)* The hardest thing for anyone is to look at their own actions and perceptions, and I personally feel you are all doing a tremendous job of staying open and receptive to the many facets of this Essence. I want to remind you, we're speaking of the Wizard in a pure form, but you are receiving it holographically, out of your experience, as you. So let me ease your concern by sharing some of the larger purposes of the **Wizard Essence.**

(Breathing deeply, Astro continues....)

This Essence *can* truly be the most incredible in the field of transformation—for these people do not just follow along or get by. By the very nature of their intensely manifestive desires, **they make sure we *all* keep moving, growing, and learning. They are our major enrollers in life, through tremendously supportive love, lightness, adventure, belief in the Self, and knowingness.**

Wizards are particularly adept at ungelling un-truth.
You may not like their methods, but if you are willing, the results can be miraculous. For they are delighted—when in balance—to share their energy with you—encouraging you to "Be" more of the Self who you were intended to be. **Wizards** remind us of our Magnificent Priceless nature and of believing in our own contribution to Life. And they support all of life as having the freedom to live fully. Truly, without the **Wizard Essence** to continually prod humanity toward reassessing its Self, humans might really be stuck in their "stupors," which have built up over the eons of being in form.

The **Wizard Essence** pushes us ahead to wake us up, despite our resistance. If Columbus had only just gone along with the thoughts of his day that the world was flat, it would have postponed the reaching of the New World. If Galileo had not held firm to the idea, even while under house arrest, that not only did the Earth rotate but also orbit the Sun, it would have postponed our current understanding of the stars and the movements of planets. If the Wright Brothers had agreed that man could not fly—then much of today's technology would also have lagged behind. So you see, the Wizard Essence encompasses both our largest dreams and our greatest fears, so that we can go forward.

In a nutshell, the **Wizard** *does it all*—but just not all the time. When it gets right down to it, the **Wizard** nature is intimately concerned with what humanity does, for the *ultimate* transformation and manifestation lies in human consciousness and awareness, as far as humans are concerned. However, because much of humanity appears to be in a habit-energy mode, it is literally in the **Wizard**'s domain to see that indeed we do grow and continue to learn. Can you see why so many public seminar leaders might be of the **Wizard** nature? The **Wizards** are the means for energy to move through. To the **Wizards,** the Invisible—their ultimate playground—is huge. And because of their intensely interactive role among humans, you can easily see why achieving and maintaining inner balance is absolutely essential to the **Wizard** nature.

(The Being and its members immediately identify with this need and drive for balance, while thinking that this is undoubtedly true for all humans—and again they collectively wonder how best to distinguish one Essence from another.)

Astro: *(picking up on their thoughts and responding without a break)* Again, it's not that all humans don't have a portion of all the Essences, but that each individual will express more constantly *one* of the Essences, in a predominant pattern. Plus, with humans of all Essences in varying stages of being **on-line, off-line,** and **very off-line,** you can see how some people can appear to be other than their true Selves. It's definitely not always clear, especially when you first begin to ponder these viewing places, but once you begin to see your own Essence more clearly, this can open the door to not only seeing others more clearly but also valuing the entire process of unfoldment, with all its ups, downs, and diversity.

*(The Being, looking over at Astro, sees the love and support in Astro's energy field, and then knows that it is **absolutely held in highest esteem in its unfoldment in life,** and the Being opens its energy arms and embraces Unicorn, Gabriella, and Amethyst Crystal, as it extends absolute love and forgiveness to its three densest means of communications on planet Earth, for indeed they had done their best, given the information they each had, to share their Being, in form.)*

(Astro, on its part, is glad to see that the Being and its dense-body representatives now realize that there is no right or wrong in learning more about their Self—but rather just the awesome wonder, a marvel really, at this incredible thing called Life.)

The world is only the visible aspect of God; **what alchemy does is to bring spiritual perfection into contact with the material plane.** *...That's what alchemists do. They show that, when we strive to become better than we are, everything around us becomes better too.*

—Paulo Coelho, *The Alchemist*
(emphasis added)

When you move energy, you create effect. If you move enough energy, you create matter. Matter is energy conglomerated. Moved around. Shoved together. If you manipulate energy long enough in a certain way, you get matter. ... It is the alchemy of the universe...the secret of all life.

—Neale Donald Walsh, *Conversations with God: an Uncommon Dialogue*

This entire program of creating miracles revolves around the simple premise that you become in the physical world that which you create in your invisible world.

—Dr. Wayne N. Dyer, *Real Magic*

CHAPTER TWELVE

THROUGH THE DOUBLE DOORWAY

(The full realization that the Being is indeed a Wizard Essence continues to come into awareness for Gabriella, Unicorn, and Amethyst Crystal, as the Being hugs all three of its dense-body members. As they review their internal catalogues of their own avenues of communicating over the years, they all see more clearly the reactions of others to their intensity of sharing their "Being," and Astro watches these realizations dawn physically, mentally, and emotionally.)

Astro: *(nonchalantly)* Well, all this *is* a revelation, isn't it—sort of makes one rethink one's life, doesn't it? What's that phrase they use on planet Earth—oh, yes: "You learn something new every day, don't you!" *(Astro grins at seeing the members still shocked at Astro's ability to read their energy patterns so clearly. For indeed, the Being, through them, has approached various situations over the years not only with overkill or excess enthusiasm, but also with an intensity unrecognized by itself as a valid "way" of being.)*

Astro: Now that you know where your "listen-ability" lies—that is, in the Wizard Essence—let me return to a more in-depth conversation about the two doorways of each Essence, so you can better appreciate which doorway, mental or emotional, *you* predominantly speak from.

127

Astro: *("pondering" how best to jump into this fair-sized pond of a topic)* Hmmm…let me start by saying that people who favor the **mentally-based** means of communicating tend to "do their love" and *listen to* the exact definitions of others' speech and the written word. On the other hand, **emotionally-based** people could be said to lean toward *hearing* Love, or *feeling* the heart-felt quality in people's tone of voice….

(Astro pauses to fine-tune and materialize an emerging idea.)

Astro: *(continuing with a flourish)* Actually, here's a *list* of many direct comparisons between these two doorways of communicating. Just like apples and oranges, which are both great to eat but have never been joined, **the mentally- and emotionally-based traits are equally valid yet diabolically opposite in many cases.** Please bear in mind that even though this list is extensive, in no way is it complete, for humans have endless ways to creatively express their preferred means of communication.

The Two Doorways of Communication: Mentally-Based vs. Emotionally-Based Languaging

On the one hand, ***Mentally-Based Beings*** tend to:

- focus mainly on the *outer world* and lean to the use of *outer-directed* speech.

- come into life in a somewhat guarded mode, with innately self-protective thoughts, words, and actions.

- be prone to *doing-ness* in Life to show their Love.

- thrive on accomplishment.

- fulfill themselves externally.

- live inside their mental "penthouse," not always thinking to share their thoughts or feelings.

- be prone to speaking in generalizations.

- learn what they want to understand via sharing the data with another.

- find it easier to see themselves through others, or focus on others' traits vs. their own, so may sound judgmental.

- be past/future oriented, not Re-Membering that life is more of a journey than a destination.

- hate to be interrupted when telling a story.

- "categorize" things and people for clarity and simplicity.

- be linear in their approach to life, as in "compartmentalizing" upsets (setting them aside during other "priorities").

- read to gather data, finding great value in facts and figures, or be technology/computer oriented.

- give 100% backing to others through expressing 100% **agreement** (when **on-line**).

- believe that understanding is the key to change.

- move into **Continual Emotional Upset**, when **at-a-tilt** too long.

On the other hand, *Emotionally-Based Beings* tend to:

- focus mainly on their *personal* experience of the world around them and gravitate toward *inner-directed* senses.

- speak from within their life experiences, and if showing upset, it is more with themselves than with others.

- come into life totally unguarded, "wearing their heart on their sleeve."

- be prone to "being with Life in the moment" to show their Love.

- thrive on happiness.

- fulfill themselves internally.

- look inside themselves to determine the world around them.

- be prone to focusing specifically on themselves while conversing.

- seek eye contact to make sure their thoughts/feeling are being received.

- use language that centers on themselves, so may sound Self-absorbed.

- speak from the immediate present moment and *must* clear the moment to move ahead to other activities.

- talk over others once the gist is grasped.

- experience *all* as changeable or mutable.

- be *horizontal* or even *holographic* in their experience of Life, as in an upset permeating the entire day's activities.

- *hear* data, *e.g.*, "being the music"—but may read to boost their mental member or explore topics of great interest to them, or enjoy the "play" of computers.

- give 100% backing to others through expressing **100% acceptance** (when **on-line**).

- recognize that words (understanding) and actions must match for a quality shift in Life.

- move into **Heavy Mental Override**, when **at-a-tilt** too long.

(Astro pauses to take a breath, and once again Amethyst Crystal takes advantage of the pause.)

Amethyst Crystal: *(feeling cramped by all of these specific* this*'s and* that*'s)* Astro, are you saying here that every *mentally-based* Being acts specifically one way, and all *emotionally-based* Beings act specifically another way—like all the time?

(Astro breaks out in a huge belly-laugh, unable to contain its Self after hearing Amethyst Crystal's specific question.)

Astro: There you go again, A.C., so badly wanting to have everything neat and tidy in your mind's eye—or maybe you're afraid it really isn't neat and tidy?

(Astro glances over at Amethyst Crystal's visible consternation) Actually, A.C., in a way, you have hit the nail on the head on how elusive this information is. I'm sure you, of all of the Being's dense body members, are beginning to realize that none of this data "means" anything. I don't wish to discount that all of it has meaning and helps humans learn about themselves; it's just that ultimately, knowing any of this will not get you clothing, buy you food, or take you from Point A to Point B. And to further complicate things, as soon as it's put into words—it's not "that."

(pausing to sigh audibly) You see, **we are talking about** *tendencies*—not aiming to set them in stone, but rather to recognize them, come to terms with them, accept them, and

finally to "get" that **we are not our tendencies**—and that at any given time or opportunity, **we have the ability to surpass our limited thoughts and feelings and become more than we thought we could be, do, have, and so on.**

Speaking just to general tendencies, you will find that the **Mentally-based** *lean* toward expressing their perceptual Essence awarenesses from a strong **decision** or **dichotomy**-orientation—in other words, viewing life in terms of right/wrong, good/bad, here/there, and so on—as if all of living is an either/or choice, with no other options or inputs to influence the outcome.

Emotionally-based Beings, on the other hand, *lean* toward expressing their Essence viewing places from **experience,** showing more compassion if they have an experience of their own that is similar to another's. Likewise, they may totally negate a situation of which they have no direct experience. In other words, the emotionally-based Being is *experience*—or lack thereof—oriented.

And it's ultimately all about balance within the Self, for each of us has both a mental and an emotional member. When a person has been operating under extreme or extended **at-a-tilt** or **off-line** conditions, it can be very hard to know which base you are talking to—as when a mentally-based person is in **Continual Emotional Upset** or **"CEU,"** or an emotionally-based person communicates through a **Heavy Mental Override** or **"HMO."**

Amethyst Crystal: (*thoroughly enjoying its role as a gadfly*) Now there you go again—throwing out more terms to remember! Just what is this about *CEUs* and *HMOs*—are we on a trip to the hospital or something?

Astro: Now there's a thought! And when you think about it, it's when a Being gets so far *off-line* that their physical body really cannot hold any more discombobulation and *at-a-tilt-ness*, that some do end up at the hospital. As I'm always saying, **you've got three ways to go regarding health.** Excellent health is always going to cost a human Being their time; however, *on-line,* it's financially cheap to invest in health-promoting habits such as meditation, yoga, tai chi, organic foods, and so on, to maintain the balance of health. *Off-line,* there are such wonderful and affordable opportunities as massage, chiropractic, essential oils, homeopathics, acupuncture, and supplements—to help people regain balance. And *way-off-line,* we have the options of surgeries, prescription drugs, and huge financial outlays. And *all* these pathways work and will help alleviate, at some level, the stress and strain of living.

(The Being and its members collectively reflect how simple Astro's notion seems in thought, yet many times difficult to produce in form. Meanwhile, they are all still very much aware that the question of which doorway the Being communicates through has not yet been fully clarified.)

*If we can get the Mental body, which thinks it knows,
to support the Emotional body, which knows it knows,
what we would end up with in Physical reality is* Synchronicity—
known to us (in our current out-of-whack-ness) as Miracles.

—JL

This is the current of the new evolution—internal.
Evolution has become internalized.

—The Global Brain

Feeling is the language of the soul. ...
Words are really the least effective communicator, ...
most open to misinterpretation, most often misunderstood.
The clearest words are those which contain truth.
The highest thought is always that which contains joy.
The grandest feeling is that which you call Love.

—Neale Donald Walsh, *Conversations with God*

(emphasis added)

CHAPTER THIRTEEN

HERE OR THERE, THIS OR THAT

(Amethyst Crystal's purple glow grows more radiant as it keeps clearing out the debris of confusion from its upset at the beginning of this gathering, by continuing to ask pointed questions.)

Amethyst Crystal: I can understand that we're talking *way-off-line*, here, but what exactly are the *HMO* and *CEU* situations?

Astro: *(addressing the current question)* If you recall, last year we did mention that some emotionally-based people operate with a **"Heavy Mental Override"** or "HMO." **This focus consists of viewing life through a filter of negative judgments, criticisms, general negativity, and limitations— primarily self-directed.** It shows up as a real bombardment on a person's self-worth, as they tend to undercut themselves in their conversation. They may have been told as a child that they're worthless, or a burden, or not capable of doing things—and now they're telling it to themselves, before anyone else can. **This override puts that human's mental member into a constant role of judgment that it was never designed to carry out.** At the same time, the mental override makes these people appear "more mental than the mentally-based," because if their emotions get accessed, they immediately run into their buried upsets, which they deem too scary to experience. Therefore, by mentally **overriding** the emotional system, the person unconsciously hopes to miss the emotional upset they are carrying throughout their daily life.

All this judgment of self undercuts the emotional knowingness of personal worth and prevents the true function of the **mental system,** which is **designed to support and back** the Being and all its members 100 percent, **100 percent** of the time. *(Astro looks pointedly at Amethyst Crystal and sees that the mental member clearly grasps the impact of this "override" situation.)*

Gabriella: *(without having asked the question, finds itself unable to stay silent)* Astro, would that mental override pattern have anything to do with my former uncertainty to express fully?

Astro: Most certainly. Even if it's not in your consciousness, you're going to operate from a protective place, if there is *any* undercurrent of upset that has not been fully experienced and released from the body. But this isn't the only upset that occurs within humans. The mental version of buried upset is what we just called *CEU*—the **Mental Base in Continual Emotional Upset.** Like *HMO,* this focus also consists of viewing life through a filter of negative judgments, criticisms, general negativity, and limitations—but in this case, **primarily other-directed. These judgments occur when a mentally-based person places a jammed-tight lid over its deep-seated emotions.** For example, this could show up as someone who just about gets hit by a car crossing the street, and then immediately tells you everything is fine, no problem, as if their life hadn't just about been terminated. Or, having just gone through childbirth, they might say there really wasn't any pain—all in an attempt to avoid the messiness or pain of expressing their built-up emotional upsets—that is, *if* the experience was really upsetting—as not all Mothers-to-be have a difficult time of it. The point of these examples is that sometimes a person negates their own feelings, to the point where the person has fooled themselves into thinking the upset has disappeared. In their repetition of conversing that "everything's just fine," they will in fact have convinced themselves that there really weren't any emotions to be experienced. The physical form—which is not designed to hold this much unresolved and unexpressed emotionality—quite likely can end up with physical pains, such as arthritis, headaches, or constipation.

And everyone's physical "holding capacity" depends on their Essence or viewing place and their life circumstances. For the Fairy Essence, there is little holding and much releasing or avoiding. On the other hand, the Angelics, due to their strength of connection to wholeness, can seem to be able to sit in a great deal of upset, abuse, lack of worth, pain, tiredness, and misery—and still appear "all together." So the Angelic *appears* to have a greater holding capacity of upsets.

Even so, this Continual Emotional Upset naturally wants to work itself out of the physical system through a cleansing expression, such as tears, but just keeps bouncing up against that tightly-jammed lid. Since the human body is porous, when you are close to one of these people, you can literally "feel" that something is amiss, even when they're telling you that "everything is copasetic."

Unicorn: Stop, please—I'm getting a headache!

(Astro stops midbreath, and all is quiet as Amethyst Crystal, Gabriella, and the Being look over at Unicorn's distress.)

Unicorn: Look, I don't know about the rest of you, but my head is spinning, first with you two *(pointing its energy field at Amethyst Crystal and Gabriella)*, as my mental and emotional partners to assist our invisible Being-Wizard-Essence to express—and now mental and emotional *bases*, and then *overrides* that appear mentally-controlled and emotionally-blocked. To say I am overwhelmed with confusion would be putting it mildly. *(turning to Astro)* Just where is all this leading us?

Astro: *(turning to Unicorn)* You see, Unicorn, we are talking many dimensions or directions at once—*here or there, this or that*—which is enough to confuse anyone. Bottom line, we are simply trying to address a way of presenting the Self that has often been labeled as *male* and *female* traits—when in actuality, they are human malfunctions that can occur in both males and females.

Gabriella: Does that mean men and women are really the same when it comes to their ability to communicate?

Astro: In ability, yes. In development, no. It's thought that this misnomer of what is a male response versus a female response began about 4,000 to 5,000 years ago, when, due to invading tribes, the men defended their people and the women nursed and watched the children. Makes sense really—but it has since gotten way out of line, when daily "protection" is not needed to grow food and raise families and do jobs. You see, prior to this division of labor, the men and women would hunt for berries and plant foods together, plus raise the children together. Of course, humanity truly doesn't know exactly what happened, but division of labor ended up in the social and cultural mores, until now they are considered "a given." From my vantage point, however, it looks like a lack of training. Irregardless—humanity is slowly chipping away at the "female's lack of intelligence" syndrome and the "male's lack of feelings" scenario.

It's sort of like that traditional "June bride" business in your culture. Not so long ago, in American colonial history, people got married in June simply because this was when everyone took their first real bath after the long winter. Today, it's evolved into a romantic notion, having nothing to do with its origins.

(The Being and its members chuckle at Astro's ability to bring humor into what appears to be a serious topic.)

Astro: *(oblivious to their giggling)* Anyway, I'm wandering off the topic, again, and would like to return to the information on these "tilting" or "out-of-whack" base communications. So here are just a few clues regarding the full-blown Mental-base in Continual Emotional Upset and the Emotional-base with a Heavy Mental Override, with the points laid out—with you in mind, Amethyst Crystal—for ease in direct comparison.

(Amethyst Crystal beams its appreciation at Astro's consideration.)

Upsets and Overrides

Mentally-based Beings, when off-line or way-off-line (*i.e.*, in Continual Emotional Upset—"CEU") tend to:	Emotionally-based Beings, when off-line or way-off-line (*i.e.*, under a Heavy Mental Override—"HMO") tend to:
• pretend to be okay despite exuding an "uncomfortable" feeling.	• fluctuate between "pulling the rug out" from under themselves and heavy denial.
• think that merely saying they are fine, means they are fine.	• think that berating themselves will keep the deep upset "at bay."
• use terms like *should*, *would*, *could*, or *ought* toward or regarding others.	• absorb negativity around themselves without realizing it until later, if at all.
• view emotionally-based Beings as too haphazard or out of control.	• view mentally-based Beings as judgmental and devoid of feelings.
• create excess weight from not paying any attention to the physical body's needs.	• create extra weight as protection.

Astro: One thing is for sure: in both cases, the person is at odds with themselves. So, until the emotional system is honored as fully as the mental or intellect (*i.e.*, as life experience), humans will store upset, at-a-tiltness, judgment, and so on—either in the physical form or in their vocal conversation. And the at-a-tiltness may show up as overeating in the physical body, as judgment in the mental body, and as withholding of love in the emotional body.

(Once again, Gabriella and Amethyst Crystal look at each other, realizing this truth from personal experience—and knowing just how detrimental this at-a-tiltness can be.)

Astro: *(stretching its energy vibration as it settles in to review this awesome awareness)* As I've said many times, **generally speaking, emotionally-based Beings share experiences from an "I" point of view.** Actually, this is one very good way to sidestep criticism, by speaking for oneself alone, and by not presuming to speak for others. **Mentally-based Beings, on the other hand, tend to share experiences from gathered research, in an outer-directed way, using "you" as a focal point:** *"You've got* to try this—because Dr. So and So says so," or "The latest survey from the National Institute of Health (NIH) says you should do this or that."

Taken a degree further, the mentally-based tend to say, *"You should* do this or that," *"You should see____,"* thus making these folks come across as **100 percent** *for* or *against* things in their conversation. When a mentally-based person is *on-line* and fully supportive, then they are naturally quite accepting of variances, because they are in touch—that is, in full, balanced communication—with their emotional and physical body members. This inner balance expresses in both inner- *and* outer-directed statements, such as, *"I* really enjoyed this book—*I* think *you'd* really like it, too."

However, when they make blanket statements, or ignore or discount others' points of view, they indicate their *off-line-ness,* as in, "Anyone in their right mind would do it *this* way!" To listeners, this statement feels as though judgment is being placed on them, or as if some part of themselves or another person is not okay or not good enough the way they are.

But remember—as we said last year at the annual Symposium of Human Body Parts, **you can deflect overriding energy that is "coming at you" by a few simple formulae.** For example, you can say, *"Thank you so much for sharing that...,"* or *"I really get that that's true for you!"* or *"Now, that's a thought, isn't it...,"* or, *"*Would *you mind saying that another way, or restating it, because I'm having trouble 'getting' how you're perceiving this."*

You see, **if upsets don't get handled out** *there*—**at the point when they happen between people—then they tend to get stored in** *here*. *(Astro points toward the Being's chest and abdominal area)* And Beings carry those unfinished, upsetting, painful items inside and replay the scenario in other life circumstances.

(As Astro pauses, Gabriella, finally at ease with the gist of Astro's conversation, settles back within its energy field and waits for Astro to collect its thoughts.)

Astro: *(scanning its Self for any further examples to share and returning its attention to the three body reps and the Being)* But don't get too concerned with all this. In the end, it's just a way to help you know who you're talking to in life—and also a way to help your Selves modulate your own inner balance. For, now that you have experienced some balance, you're better equipped to sense or know when you're starting to tilt or straying out of alignment. Just look at all the progress you all have made in one short year! In another year, who knows? Right about now, through this very type of awareness, **human Beings are moving toward the cosmic marriage of the mental and emotional bases—and their full humanity—a state where abuse is not tolerated in any**

form to anyone. And, before you know it we will find the understanding of these base systems as common knowledge and their unique expressions honored more fully in each individual.

This extended understanding will help with relationships, too, because we won't have to marry our opposite in order to experience the other base, and because we'll be working with all our members from a perspective of strength, more fully utilizing their respective roles. In other words, from now through the end of the century and beyond, we'll be experiencing a merging of these mental and emotional ways of communicating, so the distinctions will grow less and less exaggerated as more and more people come *on-line* within themselves.

*(Gabriella, after hearing all this, feels deeply certain that their Being is **emotionally-based** in its heartfelt way of supporting and encouraging everyone she meets.)*

*(At the very same time, to itself, Amethyst Crystal is clear that their Being is **mentally-based** in its full support of others and sharing of information.)*

(Astro, intercepting these thoughts, chuckles at the effort this Being's members are putting into grasping this very nonsensical information.)

(Meanwhile, tired from all the mental activity, Unicorn lays down and takes a snooze, while the Being ponders the question of its base of communication.)

"Don't give in to your fears,"
said the alchemist, in a strangely gentle voice.
"If you do, you won't be able to talk to your heart."

—Paul Coelho, *The Alchemist*

If I am out of tune with myself,
then my view of reality will be distorted.

—Rev. Matthew McNaught

You are a child of the Universe,
no less than the trees & the stars;
you have a right to be here.
And whether or not it is clear to you,
no doubt the Universe is unfolding as it should.

—"Desiderata," found in Old St. Paul's Church, Baltimore, dated 1692

The Universe is perfectly orchestrated—
only we think it should be doing something else.

—JL

CHAPTER FOURTEEN

THE HOLOGRAM OF MAGIC

(After an eternal moment, Gabriella, first to recover from all the new data, poses a question to Astro.)

Gabriella: *(steeped in certainty, but unsure)* So just which base are we?

Astro: Just as you discovered your Self through hearing of the other Essences, so can you learn about your base of communication by hearing how the two bases express through each of the Essences. In doing so, I think you'll be able to settle on which base expression most specifically relates to your Being's viewing place.

So, let's look at the mental and emotional bases, as they communicate through each of the Magical Essences. Remember, the distinction is often most visible in terms of language expression. **Across the board, you can look for the mental expression of each Essence to be more oriented towards "spreading the word" or "getting the data out" into the world, while the emotional version of the each Essence will tend to "hold the space" for its perceptual awareness.** Again, it's the difference between "doing" and "being" as an orientation in life. Also, the mental base will tend to physical thinness, due to its ability to verbally protect its arena, while the emotional base will tend to have a little more protective and comforting padding on its body frame, for safety in form.

However, remember that perceiving the base gets more difficult when the base is *off-line*, as in the mental expression in Continual Emotional Upset, or the emotional base under a Heavy Mental Override, so the "viewability" of the Essence gets blurred. In fact, being **off-base** not only disrupts the Essence, but also its ability to express through the three of you—physically, mentally, and emotionally—creating even more static on the channel. So no wonder it can sometimes be difficult to pinpoint one's own Essence and base, much less anyone else's.

(A general surge of excitement is felt by all as Astro gets ready to make this data truly spherical in nature.)

Astro: Anyway, without further ado, here's how the mental or emotional bases show up in the Essences, or what I call the **hologram of magic**—with twelve perceptual viewing places in all.

Emotional Angelic

Of all the Essences, the Emotional Angelic sits the strongest in the heart energy, maintaining belief, faith, and knowingness that any upset is not *who* we are. These are your nurturers—with cookies and milk. They will stop and play with you, even as they have other things to do. No matter what upset is occurring, the Emotional Angelic can say, "You're special, worthwhile," and so on, and thus can always build up the spirits of others. We all like having Emotional Angelics near us as friends, because they can hold such a strong knowingness of truth and God-ness, in such a gentle way. The

Emotional Angelics literally bask in taking care of and comforting others. They see everyone as whole and complete, particularly babies, who are so filled with *God-ness.*

When the Emotional Angelics "sit" in upset or turmoil for too long, they can have trouble getting out of it, because they don't back themselves strongly enough, mentally. Literally, others come before themselves in life, and if any crime is committed by these people, it's that they take on more than can humanly be done, and that they give not just their time, attention, dollars, and all—but chunks of themselves, as well! If you know someone like this—hugs and acknowledgments are very healing for them.

Mental Angelic

The Mental Angelic speaks to our self-worth and lets us know about our connectedness in conversation, by delivering data and information for us to feel connected to. Above all, the Mental Angelic seeks to vocalize the qualities of love and support. With great enthusiasm, the Mental Angelic will be found talking about love and encouraging others to come from this place, no matter what. It's this overzealous appeal for everyone to operate from connectedness that sometimes overrides another's idea of love. As with all mentally-based Essences, it's important to thank the Mental Angelics and reassure them that their contributions and drive are appreciated, if not always fully adopted.

Summary

Both the Emotionally- and Mentally-based Angelics will exhibit the quality of giving off or exuding warmth, or love, from the pores. Also, both Mental and Emotional Angelics know more than they think they know, due to the totality of Heaven-Earth-connected energy flowing through them. **On-line,** the Angelics are totally open and supportive. **Off-line,** they give you lots of advice on ways for you to improve, and **way-off-line,** they think their view the only correct one, about love.

Emotional Fairy

The Emotional Fairy runs on excitement, exuberance, and magic. These light, *lithe*-full beings are constantly reminding all of us of the play of life, and that true learning comes through play, safety, and support. Their special knack is enrolling us in their enthusiasm, and perhaps we may then see our own life from a lighter perspective. Unfortunately, many humans are so steeped in seriousness that they unknowingly drain the enthusiasm right out of these bright, colorful natures. The challenge for the Emotional Fairies is to remain in their lightness while darkness or heaviness swirls around them. If these qualities remind you of yourself or another, a visit to fantasy or magic is always rejuvenating. For the Fairy Essence, this is where the Truth lies.

Mental Fairy

The Mental Fairy, equally quick as its emotional counterpart, uses that speed to get the message out, pass data on, give out information, and share a wealth of possibilities and opportunities. If carried to an extreme, these Fairy folk end up with more information than anyone could possibly absorb, including themselves. To offset this buildup of energy, they *love to dance.* So if you're willing to dance through life with them, you will be blessed with unending magic, wonder, love, and support.

Summary

The key to the Fairy Essence is to remove debris, discord, and disruption. In so doing, they are freed to buoy the human spirit, where dreams and visions can flourish. When **on-line,** the Fairy Essence is a true inspiration to us all. When **off-line,** they'll be jittery, fearful, and extremely unnerving to others. **Way-off-line,** any sense of responsibility or link to the human plane appears to be severed, and they can look like the "walking dead," or simply not be found. To uplift this uplifting Essence, consider how it feels to visit places like Disneyland. For at Disneyland, we leave our problems and worries at the entrance and bask all day in the pure delight of living—feeling rejuvenated if not a little tired at the end of the experience. Therefore, emphasize a more creative and magical approach to the Fairy folk, and you'll be surprised at how they pop back into their human life and an ability to handle things.

Emotional Elvian

The Emotional Elvian will seem the most mischievous and speedy, while getting tons of life's errands run and friends visited. These people thrive on interacting with many different cultures and backgrounds—at record speed—and are always interested in new adventures. Their special gift to us is their zest for the thrill of living, for they recognize that each and every moment has endless possibilities of joy, adventure, mischief, and fun. If taken to the extreme, they can get very tired keeping up with all the items that they have set into motion—just like one hot fudge sundae tastes delicious, but ten can make you sick. To assist these folks from spinning out of orbit, you might suggest they take a trip to the Bahamas, leave all their toys at home, and simply enjoy the rest and relaxation of nature.

Mental Elvian

The Mental Elvian seeks out information about anything and everything, leaving no item unexplored. Their special gift to life is their ability to see so many different approaches to the same topic, forever opening new doorways and new horizons. In fact, these folks can sometimes get so caught up in making up possibilities for what they can do on a day's outing, that the outing never takes place—or it is so well-planned that even more gets done in the time allotted. If taken to an extreme, the Mental Elvians can find themselves with too many options and directions, and their focus suffers—and then they may appear irresponsible in their approach to daily life. We can remind these folks that it's okay to leave some ideas in the "good idea basket"—meaning that they can enjoy some ideas without having to manifest every single possibility that crosses their mental "hopper."

In the outer world, the Mental Elvian communicates in a way that shakes up people's belief systems, *lightly* stirs things up, and causes reactions through bringing up unconventional approaches. It playfully camouflages itself while it stirs things up, in order to wake people up out of their habits or stupor. The Mental Elves love to "tease." However, taken to an extreme, they can find themselves too visible and under attack.

A reminder to the Mental Elvian would be to refocus on its own life, allowing others to proceed at their own pace.

Summary

Remember, the Elvians are the most likely to jump "out of bounds" or to "color outside the lines"—and for the most part, this enables all of humanity to not take life *quite* so seriously. When **on-line,** Elvians hate to be bounded or predictable, and they easily dodge the bullets of conformity. If **off-line,** they can be very subdued, with their natural spark disappearing, or they operate on the attack, not wanting their world to change at all. If **way-off-line,** they may pull deeply within themselves, or their teasing turns nasty or bitter about life.

Emotional Unicorn

All Unicorns will *appear* to be emotionally-based to a great degree, which may make the distinction difficult to find. They always appear emotionally-based because belief in wholeness comes through the emotional body's realm, the *knowingness* of connectedness or love. These gentle spirits thrive on safety, purity, innocence, and pure joy.

However, the true Emotional Unicorn finds itself with very little protection from the upset and discord in the world, as the emotional base tends to "be the space" of whatever it's encountering. So, it's important that the Emotional Unicorns consciously balance their time between their inner safe magical forest and the outer world. Because this balance is so tenuous, they may lean to being more *inward* than *outward*. A truer friend you could never find, for the friendship would be based on goodness and heartfelt support. Somewhat like the Emotional Angelic, the Emotional Unicorn's tendency is to overextend energy, time, expertise, finances, and so on, on behalf of someone who as yet is not sustaining themselves, which results in considerable strain on the Unicorn's energy.

Because these Beings feel so deeply, they can literally *go numb* to daily life, so it's very important that their need for time away or time out be honored. Taken to an extreme, the Emotional Unicorn, so full of Universal Truth, can reach a place of frustration at the inconsistencies of life and literally plunge into a state of depression or explode in anger for no apparent reason. In truth, the explosion is just a way of letting off steam—but how's another person to know that?

Unicorn: *(thinking a question has actually been asked)* I know we're not just of this Unicorn Essence, but I can understand how the buildup of energy, which happens in my domain, sometimes get to be just too much to hold or explain to another.

(The Being and the others nod in agreement.)

Astro: *(deep in its thoughts and not even registering the comment)* To uplift the Unicorn's spirit, try leaving concerns and upsets at the door—and enjoying the magic of the moment, sprinkled with lots of love and support for them. The good news is, once planet Earth "wakes up" and fully "gets" the magic behind living, then these gentle spirits will feel more inclined to enjoy their stay, for others will tend to show up more kindly and humanely as the global awakening progresses.

Mental Unicorn

The Mental Unicorn is here to spread belief in wholeness on Planet Earth. It rejuvenates within its magical forest, *i.e.,* particular interest, while remaining sensitive to the changing tides of the planet. The Mental Unicorn is emotionally sensitive, but speaking through the mental doorway, is more easily able to interact with the rest of the world than the Emotional Unicorn, who is under a double-whammy, because it is emotionally sensitive *and* speaks through the emotional doorway.

The Mental Unicorn appears more secretive, because it is able to view the outside world with a little more caution and able to keep more of its deeper feelings to itself. Taking this secretive nature to an extreme, a person could live with a Mental Unicorn and never really know them. To offset this tendency of going so far within, a lot of acceptance and encouragement may provide enough safety for them to return to and share their very vulnerable self-expression.

Summary

The crux of the Unicorn nature is their hardcore belief in Universal Truth, whether humanity emanates it or not. Therefore, they will do whatever is necessary to stay linked to the heart of who and what we all are, on the inside and the outside. This absolute support in individual magnificence and the strength of the human spirit is the cornerstone of their contribution to all of life. *Is it so little to ask the rest of us to "back off" a hair, to give this Essence room to reaffirm Universal Truth?*

Gabriella: *(like Unicorn, thinking another question has been asked, responds passionately)* It seems to me that as important as each Essence *is* in the tapestry of life, *this* Essence appears to be at the basis of maintaining the individual threads of consciousness, for our Being—and ultimately, all Beings.

(Once again, the Being, Amethyst Crystal, and Unicorn nod in total agreement.)

Astro: *(having heard this statement, follows the thought)* So you can see why upping the "magic" of life experience is so critical to the quality of life—not only for the Unicorn Essence—but for everyone on Planet Earth. An **on-line** Unicorn Essence holds fast to the belief in Love, seen in magic and nature. **Off-line,** the Unicorn Essence can be left in upset much of the time, because many people are not focused on this level, and **way-off-line,** the Unicorn can go to drastic lengths—possibly even harming themselves—to pull out of what seems to them to be an empty hole.

And since they're not inclined to teasing and joking about the significance of Belief in the importance of Love in everyday life, to honor this sensitive yet purposefully strong nature—*pay attention!*
(The Being and its members quickly sit upright, thinking Astro is talking directly to them.)

(Noting the alertness, Astro beams a sympathetic smile, and everyone relaxes—a little—as Astro continues to speak.)

Emotional Dwarvian

Emotional Dwarvians are the "salt of the earth" and the "Rock of Gibraltar," so full of support that you really have to see yourself as *full value* in order to accept all the support they have to offer. This is *110 percent support*; the Emotional Dwarvian really wants you to succeed, and they simply heap understanding and helping upon you, especially if you appear to be in need of assistance. They are very evident in *being* their Love, and extremely comforting to know. In fact, they may tend to smother you with attention, they so much want to help. If you need help changing a tire, getting directions, a lift into town, or whatever, the Emotional Dwarvians are most happy to oblige. It's not hard to see how their enthusiasm could lean toward running your life for you. And you might take offense, as it may appear to you that they think you're not capable of handling things yourself. Or, you may accept all that they have to offer and lose your sense of Self in the process. But do note, the Dwarvians' interest in your life is all done with good intention.

It's always helpful to express your appreciation for their time and energy on your behalf, while reminding them that they have a whole life or universe of their own to shower their good intentions on, also.

Mental Dwarvian

These Dwarvian natures find it even less easy than their emotional counterparts to let others live their own lives. Full of good ideas, a sense of responsibility, and earthbound capabilities, to say these folks have a lot to offer is putting it mildly. Good lookers, pleasant human beings, more easily graspable than other Essences, the Dwarvians remind us of our earthly wonder in expressing our cosmic nature—of the true joy it is to be in form, even though we are not these forms. For they know that deep inside each of us is a priceless contribution to humanity. The fact that they tend to get overzealous in sharing this bit of news with the rest of us is the overwhelming factor in the mental version of this Essence. Once again, we thank them for their interest and informational input while noting that it's always best to keep one's strongest focus in one's own life.

Summary

While both Dwarvian expressions can be highly supportive in earthbound activities, they also can be equally strong in procrastination and stubbornness. As always, when our strength becomes our weakness, we are at the mercy of our own driving energy.

When **on-line,** the Dwarvians are very aware of the depth of knowing-ness that lies deep within our-Selves and Mother Earth, and at the same time they have a great tenacity for mundane and daily matters, loyalty, and helpfulness.

If **off-line,** they may become upset and frustrated with the number of human Beings who appear not to be handling their earthly concerns. If **way-off-line,** they may be highly judgmental of others and try to force them to become more "responsible" or organized in life. It's usually at these times that we can all use the reminder that "being a living example" is a lot easier for all of us to swallow and learn from, than having something shoved down our throats.

(Even though they have been highly intrigued by the entire hologram of information, all invisible ears perk up as Astro approaches the Emotional and Mental versions of the Wizard energy.)

Emotional Wizard

Just as the Unicorns can always appear Emotionally-based, Wizards are likely to always appear Mentally-based, even when Emotional, because they tend to be so very quick, have an intense presentation, and are usually very active out in the world. Bearing that in mind, the Emotional Wizards are perhaps best identifiable as deeply wanting everybody to come together in wholeness. If it were in their power, they would want to make connections, make transformations occur, and transform the world, for everyone, in a loving way. Highly idealistic, with a great belief in Magic and Nature, and full of the attributes of each Essence, the Emotional Wizard seeks to transcend upset by transforming Life into wisdom, knowledge, and wholeness for All of Life and providing upliftment for everyone, everywhere. Not surprisingly, the Emotional Wizards tend to overextend themselves on behalf of humanity, sometimes dropping into tiredness, pettiness, and overrunning the very people they seek to help. To support these folks, let them know that they are still loved, even if they are not operating from a loving place at the moment. In other words, keep what's of value in their expressions and sift out the ranting and raving that may go on while an Emotional Wizard realigns.

Mental Wizard

The Mental Wizard wants everyone to realize and recognize that transformation *is* the name of the game in Life. A key word for this person is *extreme*. Whether seeking to spread the word or inform the populace, the Mental Wizard will do so with great intensity, often dropping into judgment and point-of-view, for there is no Essence that feels as strongly about its view of life as this Essence. Taking this extreme to its extreme, these are your obsessive-compulsives, your zealots, your fire-and-brimstone messiahs. Once again, when their strength, which is the wealth of knowledge from all the Essences, becomes their weakness, the person the Mental Wizard fights is themselves, as seen in others. The Mental Wizard also is the Essence most likely to show up with an affinity for the dark side of manifestation, with black magic, or with manipulation or "misuses" of power. To support these people—*get out of their way,* and let them work it out on their level of intensity.

Summary

The key to the Wizard Essence is *power.* **On-line,** the Wizard Essence is **1000 percent** in support of people, projects, changes, growth, and unfoldment. The Emotional Wizard tends to express more through the avenue of emotional support, of confidence—and the Mental Wizard, more through informational support, of certainty in an uncertain world. **Off-line,** the Wizard nature shows up as highly agitated and impatient—with life, with other humans, and with the speed at which something is happening—and if **way-of-line,** may fully withdraw their support or go on all-out attack. Either way, you don't have to wonder what their position is; it will be very blatant. In fact, Wizards can appear quite selfish, because unlike other Essences, they *will* take care of themselves first and look to others second, which on planet Earth is not always deemed "correct behavior." Like the birthing process, the Wizard Essence *must* manifest, or their energy buildup gets out-of-whack and spills out as overrunning others, and so on.

Remember, these are your shape-shifters—people who even look different at different times. And while they are moved into their Angelic, Fairy, or other portion of themselves, they are a little easier to live with. Yet, this very ability to constantly adapt and change is something the Wizard, its Self, has to live with, as well. And that is their greatest challenge, to say the least.

(Pausing for a moment, Astro, having run the scope of the cosmos, breathes a universal sigh of completion.)

*(A collective "Wow!" is heard, as Unicorn, Amethyst Crystal, and Gabriella all come to the realization at the same time that their Being is **emotionally-based** in its Wizardry.)*

Amethyst Crystal: *(quickest to regain its nonexistent tongue)* And here I thought for sure that we were of the Mental base of the Wizard expression. But having listened to you, Astro, it is clear to me that as mentally-oriented as we seem to be at times, our base of communication definitely comes through the Emotional doorway—and expresses as tremendous support for wholeness for all of humanity—except when we are really tired, and then we sort of "close up shop" for a while to regroup.

Unicorn: You are so right, A.C.

Gabriella: *(chuckling to itself)* We really do run *hot*—and then *not!*

Unicorn: *(in total amazement)* And even I don't know when a change is to take place, until the *moment* it occurs!

(The Being is now in a bit of a stupor as it sits with the enormity of this awareness.... Meanwhile, Astro watches the Being's energy field take it all in.)

When you walk the footsteps of another,
you learn the things you never knew you never knew.

—Stephen Schwartz, "Colors of the Wind,"
from Disney's *Pocahontas*

Everyone has his or her own way of learning things...
his way isn't the same as mine, nor mine as his...
but we're both in search of our destinies...

—Paulo Coelho, *The Alchemist*

Not everybody's "everything" is "everything" to everybody.

—Debi Berbaum

It's all illusion.... Existence here, on this earth...
the reality is so different for everyone. We all make it up.

—W. Michael Gear and Kathleen O'Neal Gear, *People of the Fire*

CHAPTER FIFTEEN

DANCING THROUGH THE WEB OF PERCEPTION—TO TOTALITY

(The Being, having pondered what Astro has said about the Emotionally-based Wizard Essence, feels a sense of relief at being known in a very profound way, and of being on its way Home.)

The Being: *(thinking further on the topic of Essences and bases of communication)* Astro, does everybody fit into this pattern—of one of these twelve viewing places?

Astro: Yes, mostly, but you may not be able to get it across to everyone, for there's always the factor of the *oblivious*—that is, if a person is in "survival," he or she may be in total upset and never notice—or be able to hear or grasp—any of this. I call it the "Swamp Next to the Mountain" story.[1]

And even when people are not in "survival," they may be preoccupied with other aspects of life. After all, the invisible is just that—*invisible.* Like, for example, if you put your energy or finances down an empty hole—*i.e.,* to someone in "survival"—the hole doesn't know that it is empty. It's like doing a favor for someone who is grateful in the moment and

---

[1] See *The Body Talks...and I Can Hear It*, Epilogue.

promises to return the favor, but then forgets and/or denies it even happened.

These people are not trying to upset you; they are simply preoccupied with concerns that are more important to them. I'm not saying, "Don't help people." I'm saying it will get easier and easier to see that some people are not in a place to honorably accept your support or time or money—and are unable in that moment to show gratitude or even return the favor.

(Astro, pausing to see if any of these ideas are reaching its audience, waits a moment before attempting to clarify the Essences further.)

Astro: *(jumping in once again)* So perhaps I can review for you some of the characteristics of the Essences, but this time in comparison with each other, or by traits shared between two or three of the Essences, to better show the subtleties. For example, we can say that the "purest" trait, or the "thing" most gettable about each one could be that the **Angelics** are *Powerful Glowing Connectors;* the **Fairy Essences** are *Joyful in Lightness and Clarity;* the **Elvians** are *Mischievous Stirrer-Uppers;* the **Unicorns** are the *Gentle Believers;* the **Dwarvian** natures are the *Consistent Stabilizers;* and the **Wizards** are the *Alchemists,* the *Transformational Manifestors.*

Gabriella: *(eyes all aglow, soaking the data up like a sponge)* What lovely facets each Essence has—all representing a general perception of the Oneness.

The Being: *(interrupting Gabriella's blissful moment)* Yes, well, that is great, but what about the things you said that some of the

Essences shared with each other in presenting their viewing places? Like something about both Angelics and Unicorns exuding love from their pores?

Astro: That's right, for certain strong characteristics are definitely shared by two, or even three, of the Essences. For example, the Wizard and Elvian natures are both highly manifestive. But you find them representing constant manifestation from two ends of the spectrum. The Wizards are much more intense about manifesting, while Elvians are truly playing at what comes easy to them. And the Wizards and Unicorns are highly secretive—the Wizard as a reflection of a world full of all Essences, and the Unicorn from the need to hide itself at times in order to feel safe.

The Elvian and Fairy dynamics, when *on-line,* both exhibit high amounts of playfulness—the Fairy folk from off in the cosmos, and the Elvians on the ground. Generally, however, the Elvian nature will push the play further, to a point of teasing, whereas the Fairy nature, at that point will feel that the play has turned into pressure and will seek to lighten the energy up or remove itself from the activity.

As you have already recalled, the Unicorns and Angelics can sometimes be confused with each other because of the immense Love or Heart or emotional energy that literally exudes from their pores and voices. Only the Unicorns in general don't sustain that flow of love but rather retreat to safer ground more often than not. Likewise, Angelics and Dwarvians show high amounts of helpfulness on a consistent basis, whereas the Unicorn, while very giving by nature, will be less consistent in this arena, depending on its need to "go invisible" or retreat into its niche, or whether it currently feels safety. As in all life, this kind of comparing can go on and on until infinity, but you get an inkling of the strongest shared links or characteristics.

Amethyst Crystal: *(with energy rising)* I hate to keep sounding off about this, but just how am I supposed to remember all this!? You know me—I'm very visual—and I really *need* to see all this in some kind of a visual format. I mean, after all, I'm the one who will have to store all this data and then pull it up again on demand. So please, if it's possible, can we simplify this information?

Astro: *(feeling the increased pressure inside Amethyst Crystal)* I sense your discomfort, Amethyst Crystal, because you always want Life in all aspects neatly categorized, catalogued, boxed, wrapped, shipped, and delivered. ... However, the whole point of living is the *awareness*—of Self, of Truth, of interaction with other parts of the Whole, and so on.

Amethyst Crystal: *(quick to retort)* I realize that I'm a bit obsessed with order and form, but you did say we need to link this cosmic awareness *in form*, if humanity is to re-align its Self, right?

Astro: *(resigning its Self)* You're absolutely right, A.C. I sometimes forget that for your member to support a Being, it's helpful to have an understanding of the information.

Amethyst Crystal: *(with delight)* Thank you!

Astro: But I must warn you ahead of time. I truly don't mind giving you any of this information in a grid form, but at the same time, my concern is that you'll then try to "box in" the Essences. I must ask you to please refrain from making any of this "defined." For it's all quite like the aura, changing from moment to eternal moment. Eventually, a conscious awareness of constant change will become the accepted flow of life and seem to disappear, as we regain the whole awareness of our cosmic-and-human connection—and that time is coming sooner than any of us may think.

(The Being and its dense-body members quickly move to reassure Astro that they're beginning to catch the drift.)

Astro: Agreed, then?

(With a slight motion of its hand, Astro produces a number of grids.) So here's a brief summary of the "purest" characteristics of each Essence.

Pure Traits of Each Essence

Characteristic Most Associated with Each Essence, in Magical Terms	Angelic	Fairy	Elvian	Unicorn	Dwarvian	Wizard
Connectedness "Major Emotional Supporters" *(i.e.,* Heavenly Glow on Earth)	X					
Lightness "Keepers of Clarity and Light" *(i.e.,* Joyful Spreaders of the Word)		X				
Mischievousness "Stirrer-Uppers with a Twist" *(i.e.,* Coloring Just a Little Outside the Lines)			X			
Knowingness "Holders of Belief in Totality" *(i.e.,* Gentle Dwellers of the Magical Forest)				X		
Groundedness "Heroes and Heroines in Shining Armor" *(i.e.,* Helpful Accountability in Form)					X	
Alchemy "Intense Disrupters of the Status Quo" *(i.e.,* Quest for the Return to Wholeness)						X

(Seeing how delighted and engrossed the Being, Unicorn, Amethyst Crystal, and Gabriella are, Astro gets right into the next chart.)

Astro: And here's a grid showing a few of the strongest two-way links between the Essences.

Two-Way Links Between Essences

Characteristics Most Shared by Two Essences	Angelic	Fairy	Elvian	Unicorn	Dwarvian	Wizard
Playful		X	X			
Secretive				X		X
Stubborn					X	X
Ultra-sensitive		X		X		
Sparkle and Shine		X	X			
Manifestive			X			X
Serious					X	X
Helpful	X				X	
Love Personified (consistently oozing love through the pores)	X			X		

Astro: *(on a roll, and full of its Self)* And to further clarify, here are some of the major three-way links between the Essences.

Three-Way Links Between Essences

Characteristics Most Shared by Three Essences	Angelic	Fairy	Elvian	Unicorn	Dwarvian	Wizard
Holders of Awareness	X	X		X		
Movers of Energy			X		X	X
Lighter/Uplifting	X	X	X			
Denser/Determined				X	X	X
Heavenly	X	X		X		
Earthbound			X		X	X

Astro: If you examine the three-way chart closely, you'll see that each trait shared three ways has a representative from each of the energy polarities, and its opposite partner shows up in the opposite trait. This perfectly points up the nature of our apparent universe—always showing up as dichotomies and dualities.

Being: Excuse me—what do you mean, "energy polarities" and "partners"?

Astro: Oh, so sorry, am I getting ahead of myself again? I'm simply talking about the energy links that are most natural between the Essences in relationships. The natural polarities are Elvian-Unicorn, Fairy-Dwarvian, and Angelic-Wizard.

For you see, the Angelics, Fairies, and Unicorns, operating from the mystical, magical cosmos, are knowable as "holders" of their cosmic awarenesses, whereas the Dwarvians, Elvians, and Wizards represent the more earthbound awareness through activity, movement, and "doingness"—very similar to the distinction between the mental and emotional bases within each of us. **When each human is** *on-line* **within its Essence, being a "holder of the cosmic awareness" or a "mover of earth energy" are equally powerful,** for the dichotomy of diversity mirrors wholeness in this way.

Unicorn: *(starting to feel woozy)* I believe my head is about to spin, again. Are you saying, Astro, that the Elvian would be opposite the Unicorn in viewing wholeness—as would the Fairy to the Dwarf, and the Angelic to the Wizard?

Astro: That's right, only it's more holographic than that. You see, over the eons of time and timelessness, some of these energies have lost their full powerful presence, so that today, the **Elf-Unicorn** is like the inner circle of energy, with these two natures looking more exactly like the other than the other two pairs—meaning that Unicorns have their gregarious moments and can easily be mistaken for an Elf.

And when looking at the **Fairy-Dwarf** circle, it is larger and the two are more distinctively different in their presentations—really almost like opposites—the Fairy in the cosmos, and the Dwarvian nature very earthbound. And lastly, most evident of the personal power that all Essences have naturally, when showing up fully as them-Selves, the **Angelic-Wizard** duality is the most dynamically visible at this time on Earth. For even as they seem to hold very differing views of how to go about returning to our united Self or Home or Oneness, the Wizards and Angelics both have the power of presence to fully strive for the same results—of personal worth, goodness, cooperation, and Love in daily living.

(As the hologram of information sinks further in and resonates within Unicorn, the physical body representative feels the sense of struggle and overwhelm begin to ease out of its

consciousness, and a sense of serenity ease in—giving the
physical form a chance to sigh and let go.)

(In feeling Unicorn physically let go, Astro receives confir-
mation that the acceptance of Truth has finally reached the
densest of the means for this Being to express—and a burden
seems to leave Amethyst Crystal and Gabriella as well. After
a moment, Astro lightly interrupts the silence, inspired with
yet another way to summarize the Essences in their purities.)

Astro: And, returning full circle to the "purities" of each Essence, here are a few more "quick" ways to compare them all at once.

How Each Essence Views Life:

To **Angelics**	everything in Life is sacred.
To **Fairies**	Life is free flowing and in motion.
To **Elves**	Life is an uncertain adventure.
To **Unicorns**	Life is "at home" in the safety of a Magical Forest.
To **Dwarves**	Life is in inner stillness.
To **Wizards**	nothing *and* everything in Life is sacred.

Home for Each Essence (quality they strive for in home):

To **Angelics**	Home is in the heavens. (Home is Heaven/Loving.)
To **Fairies**	Home is in the stars, off the planet. (Home is Happy.)
To **Elves**	Home is in the forest. (Home is Friendly.)
To **Unicorns**	Home is in the magical forest. (Home is Safety.)

To **Dwarves**	Home is on the planet.
	(Home is Consistency.)
To **Wizards**	Home is everywhere.
	(Home is Diversity.)

How Each Essence Reaches "Home":

Angelics	reach Home through prayer.
Fairies	reach Home through dance.
Elves	reach Home through laughter.
Unicorns	reach Home through belief in magic.
Dwarves	reach Home through shamanism.
Wizards	reach Home through alchemy.

Trouble for Each Essence, When Not at "Home":

When **Angelics**	are siphoned off of (*i.e.*, everyone turning to them for comfort), they may become martyrs and victims.
When **Fairies**	are run over, forced to be earthbound, with wings clipped, they have no defenses; they may become "dead meat in the water."
When **Elves**	are cornered, boxed in, or curtailed, they may lose gregariousness, turn into a small child, or get nasty
When **Unicorns**	are not supported, believed in, safe, acknowledged, or appreciated, they may become depressed or wish to leave the planet, and often do
When **Dwarves**	are always saving us from our "Selves," their helpfulness may turn controlling.

When **Wizards** are tired or exhausted from over manifesting, they may lash out in all directions, have to go back and clean up the mess / pull their foot out of their mouth when feeling better.

Universal Language of each Essence:

Angelics	Music
Fairies	Color
Elves	Laughter
Unicorns	Touch
Dwarves	Nature or Earth
Wizards	Invisibility or Magic

Natural Gifts in Life:

Angelics provide loving comfort, connection, and support.

Fairies provide upliftment, sparkle, and spreading of joy.

Elves provide buoyancy, adventure, and fun.

Dwarves provide steadfastness, loyalty, and dependability.

Unicorns provide safety, gentleness, and vulnerability.

Wizards provide activation, transformation, and diversity.

Internal Contributions to Nature or Creation:

Angelics remind us of the gift of forgiveness by releasing pain and upsets and returning us to our wholeness, so we can experience it as LOVE.

Fairies are the playful Keepers of Light, Enlightenment, or RADIANCE.

Elves	are the sensors of mischief, motion, and adventure, releasing the pressure of gravity through laughter, as VIBRATION.
Unicorns	are the Keepers of the Belief in Oneness and Magic, the KNOWING-NESS behind the lessons we are designed to learn and grow from.
Dwarves	are the Seers of God-Realization in daily Earth activities and interactions, and the emanators of the security and solidarity of MATTER.
Wizards	are intense manifestors and bringers of CHANGE through alchemy.

(While the Being and its members silently ponder these "quick comparisons" and new information, Astro basks in the satisfaction that they have now arrived at a view of all of Totality, rather than its parts.)

(After much silence in individual pondering of Astro's sharings, a new thought crosses Amethyst Crystal's energy field.)

Amethyst Crystal: Excuse me, Astro, I know you mentioned this before, but are these "Essences" the same as "personalities—or how do personality traits come into the picture?

Astro: *(grateful for Amethyst Crystal's stimulating questions)* The Essence traits may show up in the personality, but they are not the personality. Personality traits are the mask, or the *modus operandi* that overlays over our true, natural, full, Self-expressing Being. In other words, the personality is the sum of the physical, mental, and emotional ways of protecting the Self.

The Being: *(it starts finally to dawn)* Oh, so these Essences are *energies* expressing as personalities.

Astro: *(to the Being)* Bingo! And by that very fact, as people become more attuned to themselves, do you realize that this conversation will be obsolete in your own lifetime!

Amethyst Crystal: *(unable to contain itself)* Well then, why in heaven's name are we talking so much about it!

Astro: *(responding instantly)* Yes, A.C., the whole conversation will be obsolete very soon, but *at the moment*, it's very timely— to ponder, converse on, and to *integrate*. For example, don't you think it's kind of funny that out of *all* the eons of unfoldment of *all* these traits in humanity, in *all* the varying circumstances of lifetimes after lifetimes, that humans don't yet seem to have gotten a handle on relating with one another—or even with themselves, in some cases.

Just think of this thing called **relationships.** Wouldn't you think by now that humans would have had that item in a little more knowable state—or at least more amenable to the people involved? I mean, just look at what occurs between family members, to start with, not considering all the other variety of close relationships that people move through in a lifetime. And yet, have you noticed that an organization, club, or some sort of group consciousness has been initiated for every item and concern on the planet—*i.e.,* save the whales, children's diabetes, mountain climbing, the homeless, ecological societies, battered women, human potential, meditation—just to name a few. But for all this organizing, have people learned to master the realm of intimate relationships—either within the Self or with others?

(As a Wizard, concerned with transformation into wholeness, this reminder really pushes the Being's buttons.)

The Being: *(getting its dander up)* So, are you saying, Astro, that we humans have been busy making organizations to help ourselves and others, but we haven't yet taken the time to clear out our own "internal closets"?

Astro: *(not one to back down)* You could certainly look at it that way, or you might consider that at any particular time on the planet, human Beings have been very busy handling the life circumstances they found themselves in and simply felt that *survival* warranted more attention.

The Being: As always, your grasp of the overview of Life is larger than mine—but isn't it about time to turn our focus inward?

(Astro, grinning uncontrollably, ends up laughing out loud, so hard that the Being can't help but join in.)

Astro: Your sincere statement of the obvious tickles me, and so—if you're willing—let's take the opportunity to look more closely at the arena of human interactions known as "family dynamics."

(The Being and its members, despite the amount of information already shared, feel invigorated from having arrived at a holographic view of humanity, as well as of their Being. Finding themselves refreshed, relaxed, alert, and ready to move ahead, they eagerly wait for Astro's next news.)

All life is sacred. ... All things have their place on the Spiral.

—W. Michael Gear and Kathleen O'Neal Gear, *People of the Fire*

A person should be allowed to develop like a rich tapestry
with all sorts of vivid colors and different moods and settings,
some harsh and some gentle.

—Catherine Coulter, *The Nightingale Legacy*

When we finally give up the struggle to find fulfillment
outside of ourselves, we have nowhere to go but within.
It is at this moment of total surrender
that the light begins to dawn. We expect to hit bottom,
but instead we fall through a trap door into a bright new world.
We have rediscovered the world of our spirit.

—Shakti Gawain, *The Moment of Total Surrender*

Our gift to Life is our selves.
Life's gift to us is the opportunity to recognize our value.

—Anonymous (found on a bookmark)

CHAPTER SIXTEEN

FAMILY DYNAMICS:
THE GENETICS OF MAGIC

(Feeling as though a sense of pressure has been removed, now that they know their own Essence and base of communication, the Being and its three dense-body members exude sparkling and rejuvenated energy patterns, as they all sit back to listen to Astro share about the earthly evolvement of the Essence information.)

Astro: *(happy to continuing sharing)* Yes, Being, it seems that Earth history has progressed to the point of a conscious awareness that inside each and every person is not only a universe in itself, but also a direct link to all of Life. And, although linked to all of Totality, human Beings are not necessarily conscious of this fact in their daily family dynamics. And yet, the Essences do show up in families and have survived, quite probably through being passed down through the children.

I like to call it the "**genetics of magic**" or *Imagenetics*™, if you will. Imagenetics has to do with the perpetuation and the survival of these perceptual viewing places that we are calling Essences. Whereas *Humanology in Motion*™ is the invisible ingredient, expressing outward from within the human Being, *Imagenetics*™ is the infiltration from the cosmos, into each person. Actually, *Humanology* and *Imagenetics* are one and the same, because they are both fully of the eternal factor—but we are pulling them apart for the possibility of discussing that which by its very nature as Totality has no distinction. Put another way, *Imagenetics*™ explores the invisible portion of the concrete science of genetics, while *Humanology in Motion*™ explores the invisible realm of human interactions.

As I'm always saying in reference to the Earth plane, it won't be long before someone gets a Nobel prize for scientifically proving that what's invisible is larger than what we see. *(chuckling at its own cosmic joke)* And at that time, *all* thinking will be freed up from the bondage of life having to be lived a particular way, which will allow human consciousness to explore the dimensions going on around it, as well as the fullness of Totality. It will be a quantum-leap shift in how human Beings hold themselves, others, and all of life on Earth.

In fact, I have a notion that this invisible element of "Life wanting to experience Itself" may be a basic urge behind human procreation, and that the magical part of us works to ensure its own survival. For, whenever the "magic" of union occurs, conception and creation takes place. And so, the bases and Essences show up in the children, no less!

From my observations, the *Imagenetic* patterns seem to reproduce in certain ways. For example, the most easily "getable," handed-down trait seems to be one's base of communication. In general, when a child comes in as the first-born of a family, it seems to inherit the same base of communication as the mother (*i.e.*, mental or emotional), whereas the second child shows up with the base of the father. Therefore, the first child will *seem* like the mother, due to its base of communication, and the second child will *seem* more like the father, even though most children appear to be emotionally-based because they haven't moved into past-future awareness, which kicks in at about puberty.

On the other hand, the *Essence* of the father—or its opposite matching Essence—may show up in the first child. Likewise, the mother's Essence—or her opposite—may show up in the second child. I have to warn you that these observations are from my own *mini-survey* conducted over the years, showing up in what appears to be a pattern. However, due to the "haze on the signal" when a person is *on-line, off-line,* or *way-off-line,* or operating from Mental Overrides or Continual Emotional Upsets, any kind of generalization is still extremely elusive to make.

Unicorn: *(Astro's words having piqued its interest)* But what do you mean by *opposite matching Essence*? Are you referring to the energy polarities and partners again?

Astro: Oh—into my Self-made languaging again. Thank you, Unicorn—I most certainly am. In this case, *opposite* means that if the father is Elvian, the first child will be an Elf or Unicorn. And if Mom is, say, Angelic, the second child would come in as Angelic or Wizard. As we talked about a little while ago, three "opposite" combos or dualities show up among the six Essences—the **Elf-Unicorn,** the **Fairy-Dwarf,** and the **Angelic-Wizard** pairings. These opposite pairs have a natural resonance or attraction, and they tend to attract and reproduce themselves or their opposite.

I know it's a mouthful, but here's the gist of it again: the first child carries the same base as the mother and might inherit the father's Essence or its opposite, while the second child carries the same base as the father and may inherit the mother's Essence or its opposite.

In terms of other offspring, it's not yet known whether the third and other children keep this "every-other" repetition or pattern of the base, with one being emotional and the next mental. But regarding Essence, in any given family, the Essence and opposite of the mother and father are the only four possible combinations, for that family. And if the parents are mated with their same or opposite Essence, then *only* those two Essences will surface in the children.

Amethyst Crystal: *(befundled)* I was with you all the way, Astro, until the last bit of data you just shared with us. Do you think maybe a few more examples could be thrown our way at this point?

Astro: *(coming out of a fog)* Oh, so sorry. You really have to watch me, when we get on these cosmic topics, because I do tend to "surf" the cosmic waves. Putting this in Earth terms, say we have an emotionally-based Angelic mother. And she falls in love with a mischievous mental Elf of a man. As a result of their love, they produce several children. The first is emotionally-based, like the mother, but has the dynamics of the Elvian Essence and shows up in form as a female. The second child arrives with the mental base of communication, inherited from Dad, and has the intensity of the Wizard Essence, picked up from the mother's recessive invisible patterning—and this second child also shows up in a female skin-suit. So, A.C., does that give you a little idea of what we're talking about?

Amethyst Crystal: You know me—I need things as concrete as possible. After all, how am I supposed to *see* it? And we are talking about translating this invisible information into form, aren't we? … In fact, that leads me to my next question. Why did both children come into form as females?

Astro: *(bemused at the quickness of thought that Amethyst Crystal emanates, pauses a moment to ponder the answer)* Hmmm. Being more familiar with the cosmic element, here, my best guess would be to say that as a universe in its-Self, each person picks the male or female form that best suits their lessons. But like most of this information, it's not set in gold, nor limited to one way of viewing.

(Looking over toward Amethyst Crystal, Astro sees that its communication has resonated.)

So let me see if I can say it another way. **When the same or opposite Essences come together in a family, we can see that all the temperaments and looks of the family members are along a similar plane**—not identical in their presentation, of course—but meaning that if the parents are paired within their natural combos, then the whole family is harmonious within its own dynamic. This occurs if an Elf marries an Elf or a Unicorn, for the Elves and Unicorns are closely matched vibrationally, like best friends.

However, in other families, you sometimes have a mishmash of looks and also temperaments. This can happen if a Wizard thinks it has run into an Angelic nature, when in reality it has located a Unicorn—because both Angelics and Unicorns have that strong loving presentation—and the Unicorn may have been in its powerful niche when the Wizard met it. The Angelic would be the Wizard's vibrational opposite match, but when it pairs up with the Unicorn, the resulting children can be Elves, Unicorns, Angels, and/or Wizards, in

Essence. In such a case, the intense, dynamic energy of the Wizards in the family can be a lot to handle, for a parent who has the more sensitive Elvian or Unicorn nature.

Gabriella: *(attuning to Astro's comment)* Does that mean at least one of our Being's parents is an Angelic or Wizard Essence?

Astro: *(with enthusiasm)* Yes, Gabriella—that's it! Have you ever seen a family photograph, where all the members of a family look identical—or radiate a very similar energy? Well, this would be a family where the parents matched up with their same or opposite Essences.

And then there's the family photo where you wonder where so-and-so came from, because the members appear *so* very different. Well, that's the result when some of the cross-matches get together. Now remember, we are not discounting biological genetics, astrological signs, or environments as factors. These too have an impact on the look and the feel of the family. It's just that there seems to be this *invisible* factor that is behind these other criteria.

Amethyst Crystal: *(starting to put these ideas into some sort of order)* You mean, Astro, that this *invisible realm* you have been talking about is like the *space of creativity*, and out of this space, as we move into form—these traits form the foundation of what it is to be human?

Astro: You are *so* close, A.C. Not only are these traits the foundation of who people are as human Beings, they are also their cosmic links to the Oneness we all are. So as these factors become familiar to us, our ability to hold conscious awareness of our cosmic divine Self—within our individual human Self—becomes a living *knowing-ness* to us and expresses in our daily lives.

I have put this *knowing-ness* into magical terms, so it can be easier to grasp as a concept. And, noting how these Magical Essences pair up, it seems that all humans have a dichotomy or duality to explore. Very simply, the pattern appears to be like this: Elvian and Unicorn parents each pass on either the Elvian or Unicorn Essence to their children, Fairies and Dwarves pass on either the Fairy or Dwarvian nature; and Wizards and Angelics produce either the Angelic or Wizard presence.

(pausing for a moment, to ground the data once again)

Another example of *cross-matching* would be a Dwarf marrying an Elf, where the resulting offspring can range between Fairy, Elf, Dwarf, and Unicorn. The most extremely noticeable cross-matches occur when an Angel or Wizard pairs up with any another Essence than its own and ends up with a Wizard child. In these cases, the driving, high-amp, high-profile Wizard energy can tend to roll right over—and may squelch the life ability, or *contributability*, out of—a lighter or more sensitive nature such as the Unicorn or Fairy. This Wizard child may literally run right over a Fairy or Unicorn parent, or even another Fairy sibling—even though a Fairy child is the most likely member of any family to *always* be "up."

Unicorn: *(having an affinity for children)* Are the Essences knowable in children?

Astro: *(not having ever thought on this possibility)* Some of the key traits may be visible in their interactions, but in general the Essence gets clearer as the child moves through puberty into adulthood, when it is less influenced by parental interaction and has a chance to move into its Self-expression more fully.

Truly, this whole new science of *Imagenetics*™ may raise more questions than answers, for certainly not all the data is even in yet, nor is it easy to pinpoint. As far as is now known, there may be endless possibilities as to how it works, because it's not limited to what any one human can hold. *Imagenetics*™ is still in its infancy as a school of thought. We don't have much data on what happens in the case of twins or triplets, for example, or as to the ways these items might show up in dominant or recessive patterns.

(Astro, as it speaks, begins to speculate to itself whether "dominant" and "recessive" patterns might occur on the invisible realm according to the lessons a particular human Being wants to learn while in form—and the timing of those lessons while in form.)

Atro: *(returning to its spoken thoughts)* As Amethyst Crystal points out so beautifully, endless possibilities can be explored. And Unicorn and Gabriella know that **the point is not *which* Essence or base a person is, but rather how a person can *get* that he or she has a unique contribution and viewing place in life, and that all others are equally endowed and valuable.** And it's the individual's *Incredible, Magnificent, Priceless nature* that is the true gift.

(Astro pauses as the Being, Unicorn, Gabriella, and Amethyst Crystal marvel at the circular—no, holographic—nature of consciousness.)

The Being: *(still trying to adapt this awareness to daily living)* So Astro, you've spoken about the family dynamics. What exactly does this have to do with personal relationships?

Astro: You see, in the areas of personal or intimate relationships, or major partnerships such as marriage partners, children, boss-employee relationships, business partners, and close friends—from the beginnings of time as we know it, each Essence was designed to connect up with its own viewing place as well as its energetic counterpart—either one's same Essence, or the pairings we talked about, the Angelic-Wizard, Fairy-Dwarvian, or Unicorn-Elvian. These *energetic counterparts* just naturally *get* you better, because they can identify with a few more of your idiosyncracies than the other Essences can, and the upshot is, their *get-ability* of you is more of a given. This does not mean we are not to interact with *all* Essences or expand our ability to appreciate the many and varied expressions of Universal Self.

The Being: *(struck by the simplicity of it all)* So why don't we just look for our same Essence? Wouldn't that be the easiest?

Astro: *(at the risk of repeating its Self)* Actually, humans do tend to gravitate naturally to similarness—an Elf to an Elf, and so on—because their perceptual viewing places are familiar, and their language may be very familiar as well. When you meet someone and it resonates, you call them a friend, immediately sensing the camaraderie and understanding. After all, people don't generally fill out an application to become friends, and they often don't even truly notice when the friendship fully emerges.

But remember, humans are on planet Earth to learn and grow, which pretty much means they are designed to seek out new life experiences, or unknowns. From my mini-surveys of humanity, it appears that regarding the base of communication, most humans *do* tend to seek out their *opposite*, such as a mental base marrying an emotional base, because that is the part of their Self that they are working on, regardless of which skin-suit they are wearing—male or female. In the past, an assertive, mental, outer-directed nature was reserved mostly for males, while the inner-directed, nurturing, emotional expression was associated mostly with the female. It is only now that humans are beginning to recognize that every one of them carries both assertive and receptive tendencies, meaning that with enough self-worth, each human is capable of engaging fully in both the mental and emotional arenas of development.

Gabriella: (*concerned about the direction the conversation has taken*) Are you talking about women being as strong as men?

Astro: That depends on how you define *strength*. Speaking strictly physically—who knows? We have seen many female athletes exude tremendous physical strength. However, more specifically, I am referring to the invisible and internal aspects of strength, as in a mother who has survived her child's death, or a child who has been on its own since long before it received all the tools that would have made that transition easier.

And what about a very sensitive male who is uninterested in playing football and has many women friends, because he truly identifies with their energies? As with all questions, endless numbers of examples and conversations may evolve. Suffice it to say that this science or conversation is *in process*, definitely not *done*.

(*getting back to the topic of relationships*)

But in terms of relationships, traditionally, *opposites attract* because it's been the only way to get both the mental and the emotional nature under the same roof. In other words, **if we**

are not balanced, we tend to attract our opposite in base and/or in Essence, so we can learn more about that part of our total Self. Yet, as we talked about before, once more and more folks come *on-line* within themselves, develop their emotional body equal to their mental member, and learn to express *bilingually*, as it were, the need to marry the opposite base will diminish. With the strides various Beings are presently taking in the area of relationships, the predominant pattern could shift in a noticeable way quite soon on the planet, possibly around the turn of the century.

(Astro, thrilled at the Being and its members' ability to link up their individual experience with this universal playground, continues.)

But to answer your original question, Being—yes, it would seem to make perfect sense to connect in close relationships with those of one's same Essence. And matched-Essence relationships *can be* ideal. However, due to people's *off-line-ness* or even *way-off-line-ness*, most humans find themselves getting a bit "ticked off" or embarrassed at those of their same Essence—because they don't especially care to see how *off-line* they themselves may be.

This is especially so for mentally-based Beings, because they look to others to *get* themselves. It's just that they're not liking what they see, in many cases!

As an example, let's take you, Being. Coming into form as a female, you discovered early on that you could protect your Self by leaning toward the Elvian part of your nature—by adapting to those around you. To you, it was a safety factor at first, to keep from being "hit" by others' points of view. At the same time, it appeared to you that certain others, whom you now know are also of the Wizard Essence, were not your favorite people—due to the way they interacted with people from such an intense viewing space.

Later, this Elvian pattern became so habitual that you forgot your full Self-expression, moved *off-line*, and like many humans, operated from a place of *survival*, causing your mental member, Amethyst Crystal, to focus on protection instead of support. This in effect made you forget your emotional base, putting your emotional member, Gabriella, into a panic.

As you can now see, the Wizard Essence was still inside of you, and it expressed its Self at times as overriding others and their Self-expression.

(The Being, still without form, blushes, and its energy field turns a pinkish-mauve color, as all eyes turn to it and the members silently ponder Astro's words.)

The Being: *(slightly wistful in its Self-awareness)* As much practice as I've already had at pulling my foot out of my mouth, I realize that I may need to do even *more* apologizing to certain people, now that I'm better aware of how I may have been perceived.

Amethyst Crystal: *(interrupting the moment, hooked like a hound dog on this relationship issue)* So Astro, just how do these twelve viewing places interact with each other on planet Earth?

Astro: *(thinking that A.C. really is a quick study)* I think we can go straight to the point of interpersonal relationship, by sharing the interaction of each viewing place with the others—in their purest, most joyful forms—even as we're aware that this is *not* the way things have been in recent Earth history.

Unicorn: *(tired and bursting in)* Hey, can we get off the topic for a moment—have a chance to stretch, do some *t'ai chi,* snooze—or whatever? Honestly, A.C., you're just a question machine, sometimes. It's no wonder you don't spend any time "in the moment" with Gabriella and I—and from all appearances, there's no end to the amount of questions you can generate!

(Unicorn glares over at Amethyst Crystal, as A.C. remembers it is here to back Gabriella and Unicorn, as well as its Self and of course, the Being.)

Amethyst Crystal: *(smiling in good humor back to Unicorn)* How right you are, Unicorn. I do get carried away in my own thoughts— making me *thought-less* of all of you. So, Unicorn, will you forgive me for getting so wrapped up in my own interests and forgetting to support you as well?

Unicorn: *(realizing its old pattern of wanting to hold on to upsets, immediately smiles, releases its moment of frustration, and moves on, too)* Of course, A.C., and thanks.

Amethyst Crystal: *(as close to being "in the moment" as it ever gets)* How about it, Astro—care to join us in some *t'ai chi* movements?

Astro: *(again moved by the members' ability to realign more quickly in the present moment with their individual truths)* I'd love to!

> *"We're family by the blood. It's up to us to decide if we can be family by the heart."*
> —Nora Roberts, *Born in Shame*

In harmony with the whole,
I find my individual freedom.

—Shakti Gawain, *Reflections in the Light*

Give your hearts, but not into each other's keeping,
For only the hand of Life can contain your hearts.

—Kahlil Gibran, *The Prophet*

CHAPTER SEVENTEEN

THE TAPESTRY OF RELATIONSHIPS

(Quite refreshed and more at ease from the rejuvenating t'ai chi *movements, Astro, the Being, and its dense-body members all gather again to continue hearing Astro address the topic of relationships between the Essences. Even Amethyst Crystal was able to suspend most of its "thoughts" for a moment, and now all are ready to listen again.)*

Astro: *(realizing that it never experiences "tiredness," nonetheless having enjoyed the break)* Since our first relationship is with the Self, let me create an image to illustrate the purest forms of these Essences, when they are each experiencing optimum support. Just imagine the *Magical Forest* for a moment. In the forest, as things were originally, the Unicorns would just relax and *be*, while the Elves would gregariously stir up any or all of the creatures. The Fairies would be busily looking for rainbows, wild flowers, or anything bright and shiny to flit around and about, while the Dwarvians would be set in their industrious pursuits, happy to be in a solid routine. At the same time, the Angelics would be basking in the light coming through the trees, bringing all creatures to them like a fountain of love. And the Wizards would be busily trying to manifest new experiences of the forest itself.

(Astro looks over to find Unicorn, Gabriella, Amethyst Crystal, and the Being, all on their backs with dreamy looks on their energy faces.)

(Astro coughs loudly to regain their attention.)

Astro: **Ultimately, all humans do have the capacity for peaceful and harmonious relating, first within themselves, and then extended out to others.** However, over the eons of time, humans have moved out of this integrated balance. I will share a little bit on how each nature relates with each of the others, in terms of the current tendencies among humans—bearing in mind that the dynamics are not limited just to husband-wife or marriage partner situations, but include any close relationships, such as parent-child, boss-employee, close co-workers, best friends, business partners, and so on.

(Jumping right into the heart of the matter, Astro begins with the Angelics.)

Angelics with Angelics

Depending on the Angelics' bases of communication—that is, whether both are emotionally-based, both mentally-based, or whether they are one of each—Angelics with Angelics will find living or working together as either *heaven* or *hell*. In a heavenly state, the individuals involved will each have their own world in which to gather and spread love, and quite likely this overflow of love will support the relationship as well. In a less heavenly state, however, great differences of opinion can arise as to how the love is gathered and dispersed. This controlling factor has the potential to diminish the love between the two, causing greater and greater riffs, which may become irreconcilable.

Angelics with Fairies

The Angelic-Fairy alliance can be both mutually supportive and happy. Since both Angels and Fairies have wings, this allows both to be *cosmic* around each other. The Fairy lightness can help to uplift the Angelic when the Angelic's endless reserves are drawn low, and the Fairy responds to the heart-felt-ness of the Angelic and picks up the validation that goes along with the Angelic's honoring of the connection, wholeness, place, and belonging of all things. Angelics will find the light-filled Fairy energy less discombobulating than the energy of the Elf or Wizard, but they may not always find it substantial enough to suit them, and the Angelic may tend to want to reform the Fairy.

Angelics with Elves

This connection can be quite fulfilling, as it contains both cosmic and earthbound factors. The Angel and the Elf can really get into the *flow* of life together, as being in motion is important to them both. However, the Angelic gravitates more toward the flow of wholeness, while the Elf just seeks motion, variety, and activity, period—so sometimes the Elf may move a bit too quickly for the Angelic Essence, or annoy the Angel because the Elf tends to be a bit out-of-bounds in its play and too teasing, while the Angel tends to be more contained and "responsible."

Angelics with Unicorns

These two both "ooze" love from the pores, so they can simply enjoy being together, basking in that love essence. Also, the uplifting heart aspect of the Angelic helps solidify the sensitive heart of the Unicorn. Out in the world, however, the Angelic is likely to be dominant in arenas outside the Unicorn's niches of safety. If the Unicorn can expand its safety zones and get out into new arenas in the world, the Angel and Unicorn pair will do better. The underlying difference is that the Angel can stand in heartfeltness even amidst all kinds of tragedy, war, disruption, and so on, which allows them to still be able to nurture and support others, in many situations, whereas the Unicorn will tend to go invisible under duress, retreating into its "magical forest." Again, due to the Angelics' gift of connectedness, and not being able to identify with feeling unsafe or "disconnected," the Angelic may become impatient with the Unicorn, and the Unicorn, feeling this lack of support, may come to feel it is less valuable than the Angelic, sometimes resulting in a lower Self-esteem and a breach in the relationship.

Angelics with Dwarvians

In this pairing, the Angelic will emphasize the cosmos, quite different from the Dwarf, whose emphasis is earthbound. Yet, both are strong in their convictions, so the solid earthbound-ness of the Dwarvian may prove weighty to the Angelic, who may end up feeling as if they are "overdoing" their earthbound aspect. At the same time, the Angelic may seem too "out there" for the Dwarf. Nonetheless, as always, the Dwarvian Essence will be very helpful in providing earthly support, especially if the Dwarvian views the Angelic as needing some earthly assistance. And, although Dwarvians don't really need any "helping" done for them, they do subconsciously look toward the heavens via the lighter Essences, for lightening up. Sometimes this feels subconsciously draining to the Angelic nature, especially if the more earthbound Essence seeks unconsciously to "get back Home" to its cosmic awareness via the Angelic's energy, instead of on its own.

Angelics with Wizards

This of course is a powerful duality, and Angels and Wizards often attract, especially when the Angel consciously lives its full power. Sometimes the opposites attract because the Wizard can look convincingly Angelic. This situation can later become quite a surprise to the Angelic, when the Wizard, if *off-line*, suddenly shows up as less than supportive to the Angelic. The Angelic, on its part, can stand on its own when dealing with the Wizard but doesn't especially care for the Wizard's constant shifting around and bombardment, and tends to want the Wizard to move into its other facets for balance, particularly its quieter Angelic mode. The Wizard, on the other hand, gets annoyed if the Angelic operates from a place of "less than" who they are or from a place of "holier than thou," and the Wizard may strike out at the Angelic's constant extremely soft presentation. For, remember, all Essences are contained within the Wizard, and their presences are designed to ease the Wizard's intensity by allowing the Wizard to shape-shift into these other viewing places.

Both Wizards and Angels are powerful *do*-ers, but they have different points of view as to what they want to see accomplished and how it should be done. The Wizards stir things up more, letting the energy fall where it may, while the Angelics emphasize flow and harmony in their activities, seeking to bring diverse parts together as wholeness, and seeking to reconcile diverse points of view, as well. The only nature that the Wizard cannot easily "roll over" is the Angelic Essence, for *connection* is the foundation of all life experience.

Fairies with Fairies

This pairing is a lot of fun and play, which can lead to accomplishing a lot in a short time—as these Essences grasp ideas and notions quickly. Or, it might just as easily lead to an afternoon of irresponsible silliness—all to the delight of the Fairy Essences involved. For the most part, Fairy Essences have a lot of Fairy-folk friends and are perfectly capable of entertaining themselves, much to the consternation of some of the other Essences. As partners, two Fairy Essences will either be highly productive, with lots of fulfilling life experiences to share, or, depending on their bases of communication—and/or if one or both are *off-line*—may pick at each other horrendously—resulting in getting little or nothing accomplished. Generally speaking, though, Fairies like their own kind. If they have any Self-esteem at all, both will tend to "rise up" their energy on behalf of their friend or mate, helping to make life easier in the safety of the magical forest of daily life on planet Earth.

Fairies with Elves

This combination is fun, fun, fun—with an *oomph!* The Elf and Fairy together may show up as giddy, glittery, childlike, open, freeflowing, unplanned, and spontaneous—and considering the Elf's "color-outside-the-lines" nature—quite gregarious. Lightness and frivolity are in the forefront of this relationship, and it can take on a definite mischievous flair, with the Elf stirring things up and the Fairy hovering nearby as a spectator, with exclamations like, *We are?? Oh, my gosh!? We couldn't possibly!!!? Oh, but we are!!!...*, and so on. Of course, if the Elf is *off-line* or in need of being in control—the Elf may push the fun past nice into nasty and cause the Fairy partner to withdraw its light and lightness. On the other hand, if the Fairy is *off-line* or appearing to be uninterested in the shenanigans of the Elf, the Elf may move into a funk. As always, the deciding factors return to the individual. When one is at peace with and accepting of one's Self, then one's interactions with life become more fulfilling on their own merits and less determined by another's actions or lack thereof.

Fairies with Unicorns

This relationship will be fine if the two can meet in the "magical forest"—meaning not having too many upsets in life. For the Fairy lightness can sometimes uplift the Unicorn out of its depression, especially if it emanates rainbows and joy and magic and wonder. And the Unicorn's safety and belief in magic supports the Fairy Essence to shine its brightest. These are the two most sensitive natures and therefore would tend to be highly supportive of each other's gentleness in the world at large. However, when the stresses and upsets of life hit, both might go running from the room, which would result in little support for either.

Fairies with Dwarvians

This, as I've said, is a very common diametric—or diabolical—opposition. The Dwarf is perfectly designed to support the Fairy. However, if it pulls the Fairy down to Earth with a succinct point of view, trying to make the Fairy more responsible and accountable for earthly activities, it may drain the Fairy's life Essence away. Danger to the Fairy occurs if the Dwarvian views the Fairy's choices and activities as having no consequence, matter, or significance. On the other hand, if the Fairy receives full support from the Dwarf in being its light-filled Self, the Fairy will gleam, glisten, sparkle, and uplift the Dwarvian nature in miraculous ways.

Fairies with Wizards

Watch out when this combination gets together, for the Fairy may feel like a leaf that has been hit by a tornado. The Fairy, being such a light energy, may not be given credence for its power, position, or worth, and the Wizard, if it directs all its power or intensity towards the Fairy, can nail the Fairy as if it were smashing a little bug off its shoulder. Again, this is not the Wizard's intent, and the Wizard definitely enjoys its own Fairy nature and lightheartedness. However, the Wizard is always changing and manifesting, and this can easily tire out a Fairy Essence, especially if the Fairy is *off-line* and not moving lightning-fast, as is its natural forte. The good news is—rarely do Fairies and Wizards spend long periods of time together. In short spurts, when *on-line,* they enjoy each other's apparently boundless energy, and the Fairy can experience 1000 percent support from the Wizard Essence.

Elves with Elves

When two Elves get together, they are likely to be so busy that they need an appointment just to see each other. Or they just get lots done in a short time and still have time to play. Truly feeding off each other's energy, these two can unnerve many people by the speed at which they function, including Wizards, if they are not appearing in their Elvian mode at the moment of encountering such a dynamic Elvian duo.

Elves with Unicorns

This pair of similar opposites shows up as best friends and companions, and they are often found sharing adventures and fun. Both emanate adventure and may look or "feel" like brother and sister, even when they are husband and wife. The Elvian is more visible about it, as the Elf's adventuring often takes place in the outer world as movement, while the Unicorn's realm of adventure may be more introspective. Tending to be more fascinated with the infinite exploration of the inner landscape, the Unicorn often prefers to remain in its own "magical forest," unless the Unicorn's niche is an extroverted one. The Elf, on its part, opens up frontiers, new and different horizons for the Unicorn, protecting and guiding the ultra-sensitive Unicorn, and alerting the Unicorn to changes in the scenario while they are out and about together. But the Unicorn, if depressed, can bring even the Elf down. On the other hand, the Elf's constant activity can at times irritate rather than uplift a Unicorn as it's meant to. In the end, the Unicorn may find its Self digging in its hooves and trying to hold back the Elf from its adventures, which will not sit well with the restless Elvian nature. At such moments, if the Elf can freely pursue some adventuring on its own while the Unicorn takes time out in retreat, the relationship can be refreshed.

Elves with Dwarvians

The Dwarf, bent on a steady, rhythmical pace, will definitely tend to hold back the Elf, whose nature is sporadic, if perpetual, movement. At first the Elf will attempt to adapt to the Dwarvian's highly repetitive routine, but eventually the Elf will revert to its spontaneous expression, regardless of which base it communicates from. The Elvian, if late for the movies, automatically picks up the pace, whereas the Dwarf, being the personification of consistency, rarely varies its speed or routine for any reason, including the start of the movie. Because of the diversity in these two Essences, lots of lessons unfold for the individuals involved; however, as we notice in human life, more learning may occur in disruption than in harmony, so who's to say that any combination is less than "ideal" for the parties involved.

Elves with Wizards

This pair has a natural sharing of manifesting, motion, and stirring up of the status quo. However, the Wizard is more serious about the activity of manifesting, while the Elf's eyes may tend to glaze over at some point around the Wizard's ceaseless agenda, because the intensity of the Wizard takes more energy than the Elf wants to invest. The Elf can put out a little more energy for short spurts, however. Difficulties come, as usual, when the Wizard is off-base or out of balance, for it can entrap or shoot down the less intense Elf, even without intending to. On the other hand, as is true with virtually all Essences when interacting with the Wizard, once overridden, the Elf will tend to withhold its Self and its love—the very heart of any relationship.

Unicorns with Unicorns

This pairing just doesn't seem to occur much on planet Earth yet. For, imagine if their niches are different—and they are bound to be—then who will there be to provide safety for whom? It's sort of a Catch-22 on a planet where belief and safety are not yet considered a given. However, *just imagine* two Unicorn Essences who have the ability to take safety *wherever* they go, spreading the belief in magic, which truly opens up all possibilities for this and all other unions. This indeed is the secret of their immortality in myths and legends.

Unicorns with Dwarvians

The depth of feeling in both the Dwarvian and Unicorn Essences makes this union a very profound one. Each partner, strong in their particular beliefs and the way in which to share these beliefs in the world, holds firmly to that particular viewing place. The level of consciousness of each partner will determine whether this pair are highly supportive of each of their domains or whether they are combative in nature. The Dwarf can hold its own and function securely in itself in all earthly situations, while the Unicorn may feel unsafe in some human interactions. Nonetheless, the Dwarvian will tend to want the Unicorn to muster up to the Dwarvian's level of earthly activity. While the Dwarf will be saying, "Get real!" or "Stop trying to live in a fantasy world," the Unicorn will be saying, "The Earth is not all there is … let's open up to some cosmic possibilities." Once again, this relationship offers much room for growth to the participants involved.

Unicorns with Wizards

This combination can be highly beneficial to both the Unicorn and the Wizard, especially if it relates to the Unicorn's niche. As you might recall, when in its niche, the Unicorn is quite powerful, and the Wizard loves to engage in life on this level. However, in a close personal relationship, quite likely the Unicorn is going to move in and out of its niche. While "out," the Unicorn may feel the Wizard's frustration in wanting to remain at the intense level that the Wizard pre-fers—and therefore the Unicorn may end up feeling ex-tremely unsupported. So, much like the Fairy-Wizard con-nection, shorter spurts of contact are most likely to foster the longevity of this relationship, at this time on the planet. For, even when the Wizard is in its Fairy or Unicorn mode, it doesn't stay there long—and it brings its intensity wherever it goes. Remember, the two most sensitive natures are the Fairies and the Unicorns, so not surprisingly, the Wizard energy really is a bit much, much of the time, to them.

Dwarvians with Dwarvians

Believe it or not, these folks really do like to interact with their own kind. After all, these people are very aware of the Earth plane, and there is lots of activity and awareness going on here. The difficulty might come when one or the other gets a notion and believes that it *must* be followed—and then attempts to push the other in that direction. In such a case, quite likely no one will gain ground—and a standstill ensues. The good news is, if *on-line,* the Dwarvian Essences are well-attuned to Oneness, through going deep inside themselves and the Earth—and reconnecting to the Cosmos, where they both benefit.

Dwarvians with Wizards

Wizards may be attracted to Dwarvians due to their steady pace, security, and predictability—which is so opposite to the Wizard's general nature. However, at the very same time, Wizards may have difficulty with the routine and mundane sameness of a Dwarvian's pattern. Truly, Wizards need to manifest and thrive on diversity, even as they crave stability.

The third-dimensional, material orientation of the Dwarf, if truly aligned within its Self, may be able to provide a home base from which the Wizard can operate. The strength of this relationship tends to center on concrete earthly activities, such as going to dinner, getting the groceries, enjoying music at the park, and so on. However, should either move off-center, each will have met their match in stubbornness in holding to a particular point of view. Crazy as it sounds, though, both the Wizard and the Dwarf can be known to enjoy this locking of horns.

Wizards with Wizards

Like all Essences, when paired with their own kind, both their strengths and their weaknesses are magnified, and this notion particularly holds true for the Wizard-Wizard combo. As with the Angelics, this pairing can be heaven or hell to the Wizards involved. All of daily living is intensified within this pairing, for both parties operate from high intensity, even when they're low. And even in normally mundane matters, such as conversation, the sparks are likely to fly, much like fireworks. Once again, the base of communication and whether the partners are *on-line* or not has a great deal to do with whether these folks get along or push each other "over the edge." In truth, the saying "never a dull moment" easily applies here, as the generative, manifestive nature of both people will establish the norm or basis for the relationship. Also, depending on whether this is a parent-child, work-related, or personal relationship, which would determine the amount of time actually spent together, the fiery dynamics will be less impactful in some cases.

One thing is certain—the intensity of two Wizards in interac-tion can work to manifest both life lessons and accomplishments at a level and rate that might make others, of different Essences, flee the scene. However, such intensity, as you know by now, is very much suited to the Wizard's nature, so the goings-on may make the observers uncomfortable, while the Wizards will be in their element as they "do battle" with each other or "go at" transforming life.

(Astro, having provided a brief glimpse into every possible pairing between the Essences, suddenly finds its Self emptied of thoughts—at least for the moment—on how the various combinations relate, and falls into silence, feeling a sense of completion.)

Unicorn: As far as I can tell, Astro, you are saying that there's not a better or worse, just different possibilities, when these Essences interact. Is that correct?

Astro: *(still reflecting on all the combinations of interactions)* You've hit the nail on the head, Unicorn. And I'm finding that it's just tough when using words, to keep *judgment* out of the conversation, in terms of having one or another Essence or connection come across as sounding "better" or "worse," when actually all are equal in potential for unfoldment—just different.

Gabriella: *(quite engaged in the array of possibilities)* Speaking of judgment, it seemed to me that our nature, the Wizard Essence, may seem to promote judgment, by its intensity. Is there anything more you can tell us about this quality, for our clarity?

Astro: Perhaps I can give you just a little more information about the Wizard energy, when relating with any of the other Essences, to give you a broader scope of understanding. The thing that has to be remembered is that Wizards are not content just to *be*—their tendency is to change rapidly to another mode. Their partner, even an Angelic or Elf, has to be open-minded to appreciating the dynamics, transformations, and change-ability of a Wizard. Wizards themselves don't even always know where they're going to land next.

Wizards, when *on-line,* have the natural and unique ability to adapt and to support all the other Essences, each from their own viewing places. They can play with the Unicorn in its magical world, move and adapt as quickly as the Elf, and "handle" earthly matters with a Dwarvian. At the same time, they can flit merrily around with the Fairies, bask in the heavens with the Angelics, and—perhaps hard to believe—enjoy time to themselves. However, *no one* will feel comfortable around the Wizards when they are *off-line,* for they can and will flick off a Fairy, defy a Dwarf, overcome a Unicorn, entrap an Elf, challenge an Angelic, and do outright battle with another Wizard—and that's where the appearance of judgment, limitation, and negativity creeps in.

(The Being, trying to digest all of this information regarding its new awareness of each Essence, along with appreciating its Self as a Wizard, ponders its presentation of Self through-out the years.)

A correct relationship to your self is primary,
for from it flows all possible correct
relationships with others and with the Divine.
—Ralph Blum, *The Book of Runes*

Say it loud, say it clear,
You can listen as well as you hear;
It's too late, when we die
To admit we don't see eye to eye.

—from "In the Living Years" by Mike & the Mechanics

Genuine love not only respects the individuality of the other
but actually seeks to cultivate it, even at the risk of separation or loss.
The ultimate goal of life remains the spiritual growth of the individual,
the solitary journey to peaks that can be climbed only alone.

—M. Scott Peck, *The Road Less Traveled*

What is required is a willingness to look deeply at
one's present moments, no matter what they hold,
in a spirit of generosity, kindness toward oneself,
and openness toward what might be possible.

—Jon Kabat-Zinn

CHAPTER EIGHTEEN

MOVING OUT OF DUALITY

(The Being wonders just how all of its discombobulation in intensity has not landed it in the hospital, recognizing that indeed this Wizard quality of stirring up energy has permeated not only its Self but many of its relationships in this life.)

Astro: *(responding to the Being's unasked question)* It *is* a wonder, isn't it. But you see, in the cosmos, it is said that when a spiritual Being's energy is unaware of its effect on another person, it is in a "period of grace"—where its actions are noted but not sent back tenfold. So, if you are looking, Being, to all of the times you miscued and overrode another, please remember that it was not your *intent* to harm another—even if that is what happened—and the Universe noted it as such.

(The Being quickly looks up and over at Astro, with tears in its invisible eyes, at the gesture of compassion so graciously shared by Astro.)

Astro: *(smiling in return)* Regardless of how you hold yourself, Being, here are some basic truths. We will all be uplifted by the ability to accept an Essence for its inherent worth, along with an appreciation of our own Essence. We will also be assisted when feeling confidence and Self-worth in expressing the Self during times of frustration, sadness, or loss. And by so doing, we will find we have more in common with "others" than we thought humanly possible. Also, certain factors enhance any relationship—for when support, acceptance, gratitude, and kindness are shown, the other person naturally wants to respond, because God or Totality shows up as Love, Understanding, and Compassion, in any circumstance.

(Bringing this awareness back to earthly practicalities, Astro turns his attention to the Being's three densest means of expressing its Self in form.)

Amethyst Crystal: *(not one to let a question remain unasked)* Does this mean, Astro, that everyone is headed towards this union?

Astro: *(equally glad to respond)* Ultimately, yes, A.C., but the speed at which an Essence reaches this conscious awareness is entirely up to them. *(Astro stops to ponder another factor that affects relationships as well as the "journey home.")*. Besides, during this journey "home," each of the Essences has a certain *forget-it* **factor** in any relationship that may affect its progress. A relationship can have a hundred or even a thousand factors going for it, with one person having many characteristics that the other likes, admires, and enjoys, but if this *one* key factor is missing, then the relationship *won't work*, because it won't match the basic belief system of that Being's essential viewing place.

(All nonexistent eyes and ears await further explanation.)

Astro: *(taking the unspoken cue)* In other words, for a **Unicorn,** the relationship won't work if they experience a *lack of safety* when their partner discounts their basic belief in any way, through judgment or dismissal. For an **Elf,** the relationship won't work if there is *no element of fun,* of making life into a game, or if there is no allowance for being an adventuring individual, the results of which can then be brought back into the partnership for mutual enhancement. But the Elvian *must* be allowed some freedom to explore things on its own. A **Fairy** cannot sustain a relationship that is *not light and sparkly* in some aspect, and it needs to be honored and supported in its contributions of lightening up the situations of life. For the **Angelic,** the relationship must have a *sense of connectedness or Love* and be based in kindness and gentleness, and the **Dwarf** must be able to find a *grounded factor* in the relationship or project, a sense of earthbound responsibility. Finally, for the **Wizard,** an activity or relationship will not work if the Wizard is *blocked from manifesting* or is limited to only one means of Self-expression..

Basically, relating with others boils down to knowing the piece of yourself that allows you to be able to fully merge with another person. Conversely, it requires recognizing any piece of yourself that you are holding on to that is keeping you from having the experience of Oneness with others. Otherwise stated, not being able to connect through relationship with others is the act of not allowing the Self to see your Self beyond your immediate form. So, listening to one's own languaging about Life—in the form of inner thoughts as well as spoken words—provides a perfect reflection of one's state of inner balance and freedom, or stuckness and blockage. For example, the "withholding" of Self shows up verbally in humans whenever they restate guarded, negative thoughts, which keeps any Essence stuck and blocked in that particular aspect of their life.

Amethyst Crystal: But what is that "piece" of the Self, the thing that keeps some people choosing to limit themselves rather than clearing, cleansing, and revamping their viewing place?

Astro: Well, sometimes it happens when we put another person's point of view ahead of our own Truth and our own path in our life. If you think about it, this heads us toward sure disappointment. Another factor is that humans are, in general, still learning how to take care of the Self *and* stay in relationship instead of ignoring, blocking, or withdrawing from it. In this process, miscues in communication often catch people short, as when they use a word that means something to themselves, such as *commitment*, and assume it means the same thing to another person. Miscues also occur when one person lets another define the standards for a friendship or relationship, only to discover down the road that the other person doesn't value the gift of the relationship as highly.

Gabriella: *(in a bit of a quandary)* So how can we tell what another *means* by what they say?

Astro: *(feeling Gabriella's uncertainty)* Often it's a matter of looking to a person's actions—to see how another holds or backs the meaning of their words—because words without action mean very little. And this aspect of character isn't often something that can be known instantly—it can only be proven over time and experience by relating with another. **True value in a relationship is experienced when actions are present to match the words of the speaker.** Also, when miscues are realized, *i.e.*, when another's actions don't seem to match either their words—or what one thought the other meant by their words—then the ability to fully stand in one's own truth, communicate it, and receive the other's truth become the deciding factors as to whether the relationship can progress. Sometimes opening up to communicate, staying vulnerable, and *not* withdrawing can provide enough real presence and love to inspire both parties to keep going. Or, perhaps the partners can appreciate that a *forget-it* factor is at work, and back off that track until a moment when each can reassess the situation.

Amethyst Crystal: *(jumping ahead to yet another question)* But aren't conflicts or concerns bound to arise in any of the relationships, even the so-called "good" matches?

Astro: *(responding right away)* Frustration often occurs in relationship when one person moves or grows a little quicker, and then that person thinks the other ought to be moving faster too. And there are endless examples of the frustrations and irritations that can be felt. But the thing to remember is that the people we are relating to, and our feelings that occur in relation to those folks, are first and foremost *Self-evident.* In other words, **the people and events in our lives show us** ***ourselves, our feelings,*** **and they indicate** *our hidden feelings about ourselves.*

For example, you can think of any person or item toward whom you feel irritation or frustration on any account. By "going within" and engaging in an inner dialogue with that energy, you have a chance to get to exactly what aspect of that person or item irritates you—what upset is being activated in *you* about that situation. Notice what *you feel* being activated within *your Self*, whether it be "about to explode," "angry," "out of control," "frustrated," "ready to bolt," "scared," or whatever—because the other person is showing you what is true for your inner Self. Once seen, we all have the opportunity to make changes, as *we* are the only person any of us can alter in any way. Not another, only *our Selves*. When we can adjust the energy within our Selves, lo and behold, we find that the other person seems to adjust, too.[1]

This scenario is common in reference to being "in love"—or in reference to past disappointments "in love." Perhaps when someone is out and about, they see two people holding hands or kissing, and they might respond with an expression, thought, or feeling of disgust, judgment, or criticism: "How inappropriate—in public, no less!"—while in truth, they are longing for that very experience of safety, love, and connectedness, within themselves.

Unicorn: *(seeing the gift of life in a new light)* I guess I can see, with so much cross-matching and lack of appreciation and support, why some people go to great pains to avoid or withdraw from relationships—particularly if it seems to them to get to where "it's just too painful" to connect.

Astro: *(delighted at Unicorn's deductive reasoning)* That's very true, Unicorn—because when *our universe*—the world in which we function daily—is infringed upon in any way or another, it *really* hurts! So then the question becomes, *how can we connect up?* For, when energy isn't cleared between folks, or the situation resolved, even though we may not be in physical contact with the other person or group, the unresolved energy, in the form of thoughts and feelings that we're carrying around with us, continues to live, to brood, and to multiply inside *our* universe, inside of us. So the situation is over, but it's not really over—because the energy from the

---

[1] Again, information on adjusting energy within the Self or internal viewing screen is contained in *The Body Talks...and I Can Hear It.*

actions, words, or thoughts are still wandering about inside our personal universes, and *these* are linked *invisibly*, whether we are conscious of it or not.

(Gabriella and Amethyst Crystal look to each other in greater appreciation.)

Again, here's where the three of you—Unicorn, Amethyst Crystal, and Gabriella—come into play. As you've all learned over the course of this last year, you first have to clear out the "garbage" that has been gathering in your own avenue of expression—such as judgment, lack of value, or withheld communication. And then it is possible to reaffirm your truth—of contribution, assistance, and interrelatedness—on behalf of your spiritual Being, to fully Self-express.

Unicorn: *(quite fascinated with this Essence business)* But aren't we likely to be "in relationship" with many examples of each of the Essences, during the course of a human life, or even at any given moment?

Astro: *(enthusiastically)* Exactly, and because of that, it helps us all to appreciate all the viewing places. The more we support our Selves for being our Selves, the more we support others, through being "living examples"—the living proof of our understanding and valuing of all the diverse viewing places—then the more others are "freed" to do the same.

Amethyst Crystal: *(voicing a thought that has been forming)* Well, I am known to come up with quite a few "great ideas" for the other members and our Being to consider implementing—but sometimes it takes more than just one Being to carry out my visions. I mean, in terms of "enrolling" or "enthusing" some of these other Essences about our plans—is there anything you can share that might be helpful? I mean, on a practical level.

Unicorn: *(quite proud of its-Self)* I think I can speak to your question, A.C. For it makes sense, doesn't it, that just as certain things will always disrupt a relationship for each Essence, certain things will likewise always help to pull each of the Essences into a point of enthusiastic participation. That is—given what you've shared with us, Astro—certain things would just make sense to do. For example, by appealing to an Elf's sense of play, mischief, or freedom—wouldn't that draw it into the team or plan?

Astro: *(really enjoying the members' grasp of the subject)* Absolutely. And in terms of freedom, the Unicorns and Fairies— and Wizards—also chafe at curtailment, so include aspects of freedom in one's attitudes, conversations, plans, and actions to appeal to these folks. Along the same lines, the Fairy and the Unicorn are both so light and gentle in presentation that their point of view is sometimes *not heard.* So truly listening to them and valuing their thoughts can reassure them and make them feel included. To coax a Unicorn out of its niche, play up the magical, playful, and safe aspects of the venture at hand.

In reference to both the Elvian and Wizard Essences, leave room open to approach the project from many diverse possibilities, even if all are not included in the eventual outcome of the project. And for the Angelic, be sure to show how the venture connects to all of Life and how it will benefit children or the planet or nature or animals—and this nature and animal aspect will be of great appeal to the Unicorn also.

(All three dense-body members and their Being stop to look around the beautiful magical forest they are in.)

Astro: *(fully warmed to the topic)* Likewise, to attract or persuade a Fairy, keep things light and playful, sparkly, fun, and even *silly*—and there's a good chance the project will get done quickly and easily. And to attract a Dwarf, emphasize responsibility and the practical or helpful aspects of the project. This same helpfulness can attract an Angelic, if the project includes a sense of flow, connection, caring, community spirit, or personal connections. Then, to enroll a Wizard, bear in mind that they thrive on diversity, being their own boss, "moving mountains," and the freedom to attack the project intensely from any angle. After all, they are not *trying* to be intense; they *are* intense, and that is something they have to live with every day, while you might only see them once a week.

Astro: *(looking directly at Amethyst Crystal)* A.C., I'd say this is the nitty-gritty that you've been looking for all along, because having an appreciation for a person's essential viewing place, or Magical Essence, as well as their mode of communication—as mentally- or emotionally-based—really can help out in day-to-day, third-dimensional living experience—the goal being that each Essence be powerful in their own right. So, besides all the ways to reach each Essence, in many cases it comes back to such universal relationship healers as Love, Acceptance, Gratitude, and Support. Bottom line, *all* the Essences need and respond to *support, support, support*—from within themselves, for themselves, and for others—hence removing the focus on separation and returning it to wholeness. On a very get-able line, Being—if I asked you to hold out both of your energy hands toward me, and I told you I would be cutting one off—which one would you keep?

The Being: *(pondering what answer Astro is looking for, replies sheepishly)* The left one...?

Astro: *(raising its nonexistent eyebrows)* Oh really—you mean to tell me you would be okay with losing one of your energy hands—as if you wouldn't feel the loss?

The Being *(quick to respond)* Of course I would—but we are only talking theoretically, right?

Astro: Your mental member *hopes* it is only theoretical, but imagine it emotionally and physically—would you willingly give up either hand?

The Being: *(beginning to see Astro's point)* Of course not; I want to keep them both, because I am strongly connected to and value each of them.

Astro: *(beaming)* Exactly, and by that very connection—you don't even consider separation as an option, but rather focus on how to make your entire energy form or "universe" work harmoniously, in health and well-beingness, with all that you see and come into contact with.

Being: Of course—that's a given.

Astro: Maybe for you, but not for all spiritual Beings in human form. This idea gets back to the "fish in water" analogy. To you, the water is connected, and you operate as such. To many human Beings, however, the water is neither connected nor supportive, and survival or separation is the focus.

On the individual end of it, Being, is the knowledge and knowingness of your particular point of view, through which you share the cosmic awareness, as you know it. **From the joined cosmic and human view, the sense of isolation and separation dissolves, along with duality, into a perception of mutual support.** Such awareness has been on planet Earth in the past and is resurfacing again at this time, with a greater awareness of the link between invisibility and visibility, formlessness and form, the cosmos and the Earth plane, and ultimately, our Self with all of Totality.

(Astro stops to take a breath as it realizes it was so "into" its conversation that it literally forgot to breathe, and for the moment, all is silent.)

The Being: *(in union with Amethyst Crystal, Unicorn, and Gabriella)* Astro, where do you get all this information—I mean, how do you *know* it?

Astro: *(getting a chuckle out of the question)* On our plane of existence, believe it or not, we have classes in *Humanology* to assist us in entering and working with these realms. *(Astro grins broadly.)* After all, you wouldn't want us to be totally unprepared for dealing with humans, would you?

(abruptly changing the focus) Say, isn't it about time for the Annual Symposium of Human Body Parts to convene this year? Not being in time, I sometimes forget the timeline and must rely on cosmic time, which is always "about now."

The Being: Oh, yes. In fact, we were wondering if there would be any other Beings in attendance this year.

Amethyst Crystal, Gabriella, and Unicorn: *(chiming in enthusiastically)* —Or other body members like us?

Astro: *(full of optimism)* I am sure you all would see quite a change. Are you inclined to go?

(In unison, a huge, eager YES *nearly knocks Astro off his cosmic perch.)*

(With that, Astro gets up and makes a motion to usher them all in the "direction" of the Annual Symposium of Human Body Parts.)

We look not at the things which are what you would call seen,
but at the things which are not seen.
For the things which are seen are temporal,
but the things which are not seen are eternal.
—Madeleine L'Engel, *A Wrinkle in Time*

It is only when man is aware of his humanness
that he will be competent to recognize his divinity.
—Sathya Sai Baba

...The idea of learning through opposites will be replaced
with a knowing system that sees all lessons as equal.
—Jamie Sams and Twyla Nitsch,
Other Council Fires Were Here Before Ours

If we are to save ourselves and this magnificent home
we are so utterly dependent upon, we need to become a global society,
awake and aware, and willing to work together in a new atmosphere
of love, responsibility, and higher consciousness.
—Schim Schimmel

COMING HOME TO THE SELF

(All three of the Being's dense-body members, Unicorn, Amethyst Crystal, and Gabriella, are anxious to see just how similar or different the Symposium seems, given their year of journeying into the invisible realms. At the same time, the Being is a little apprehensive, as it was the only Being at last year's program, and it still feels unsure as to how to recognize other Beings—not being sure exactly what kind of an energy a purely spiritual Being emanates.)

(As they all gather near, Astro pulls them out of their internal quandaries.)

Astro: *(with enthusiasm)* It's really great to be back! Don't you think?

(As each body representative and the Being focus on the crowd before them, a light of awareness goes off inside each of them.)

The Being, Gabriella, Amethyst Crystal, and Unicorn: *(in unison)* Wow! Look at all the Body Parts, and many have brought their "Being" along—and look out there! Is that some Body Representatives with them as well?

(Silence falls as each reminisces about last year's experience—for, just like popping corn on a stove, last year they

were the lone kernel of corn to have popped, and this year it's as though many Beings have "popped," and so it would quite naturally follow that those Beings' own Body Representatives would be here to release and realign their thinking, feeling, and actions on behalf of their "Being." What a fabulous occasion!)

Astro: *(whispering so that only the Being can hear)* Was this not your ultimate desire, Being?

(The Being, stunned by coming full circle from confusion and separation into clarity and harmony, marvels at how Astro was able to remember its earlier pondering, and realizes that it is not only on its way home, but is Home.)

Astro: *(now speaking loud enough for the Being's members to hear as well)* You ought to be proud of your Selves, for out of your year's emergence into inner truth, you found wisdom; and out of wisdom, you found union; and out of union, you found all of life…as one connected vibrating energy, known to all as Love. And even though you know you're not "done" unfolding moment-by-moment, having engaged in this process for only one year, just look at the impact your shifting has had on other Beings, ways of communication, and individual body parts!

(At that moment, Foot, the host of last year's Symposium of Human Body Parts, scurries up to catch Astro before Astro disappears again.)

Foot: *(thrilled at its good fortune)* Oh, what a delight to see you again! I had almost lost hope that I might ever get the opportunity to thank you again for rescuing me at last year's Symposium. I so wanted to thank you in person for providing the opportunity for all of the participating Body Parts to be heard and responded to. As you can see, many of the same parts are here again, this time with their "Beings" in tow, and many with their Body Representatives as well. What a tremendous response, and although I am not the host this year— I was asked, if on the off-chance I found you, to ask if you would say a few words at the start of this year's Symposium. You will do it, won't you?

(Foot gazes imploringly up at Astro, who nods in agreement and excuses its Self from the Being, Unicorn, Amethyst Crystal, and Gabriella, who then hurry to find seats as the crowd settles down expectantly.)

Thumbnail: *(from the podium)* Thank you all, for taking the time to join us at this year's Annual Symposium of Human Body Parts, and welcome!

You may not be aware of the fact that this is the first year that the Fingernails and Toenails have been included, as we were always considered to be "dead" areas on the Body, but thanks to Astro, our opening speaker today, last year's Symposium took on a life of its own and enabled the organizing committee to see that even death and life are connected in both cosmic and human terms, "in a circle that never ends," on Planet Earth, just like the seasons. So without further ado, I am honored to introduce Astro, an Astral Body Therapist. Astro?

(As Astro approaches the podium, all of the Body Parts from last year's event rise up out of their seats and give it a "floating" ovation—almost deafening the Ears in the auditorium.)

(Astro, deeply moved, begins to speak as the applause simmers down.)

Astro: Words cannot fully respond to this feeling of adoration you have given me. But like Gibran's *Prophet, "Was I not also the listener?"* For centuries, human life has focused outside its Self for all its needs, yet found that the hunger of the spirit is like a thirst that cannot be quenched with material wealth nor satisfied through another. For whether you are Body Part, Being, or Body Representative, you are each linked to a spiritual Being with its own viewing place or perception of life—which I call "Essence" or the "invisible realm."

And we all have the means to know exactly when that viewing place is clean and clear and open and receptive—and when it is not. For when it is not, human Beings tend to isolate or separate themselves from the rest of life, and by my observation, this appears to be quite painful at times. So to see you all here together fills my heart with glee.

You are each your own presence, and at the very same time, you are one in awareness. To me, that is the most profound way of saying that you are living in both your cosmic divine nature and your human loving nature, linking all earthbound thoughts, feelings, and physicality to possibility, love, and manifestation on the cosmic level. I, for one, applaud you— your growth, your inspiration, and your courage to be your Self, whatever you deem that to be, with no Body Parts, no Beings, no Body Representatives left out.

(Taking a moment to really connect with all of the energy in the audience, Astro feels its heart filled with awe as it truly applauds the whole auditorium.)

(As wonders never cease, the Being finally "gets" the whole point of the year's experience and the point of Life itself—that just like those spokes on a bicycle's wheel, everyone and

everything is directly linked to wholeness, and each is here to express that wholeness, that Oneness, in a very unique expression that is entirely up to them—that, quite simply, Home is Everywhere, inside Everyone, as the Self. The Being basks in the stunning realization of what a wonder Life is, always has been, and always will be—just as human Beings, plants, animals, the Earth, and "inanimate" objects are, always have been, and always will be—Incredible, Magnificent, Priceless Gifts.

(And, as all the members of the audience spontaneously hug each other in acknowledgment, Astro slips away to parts unknown, where another planet, facing its own ordeals, awaits its arrival. Truly, an Astral Body Therapist's job is never done.)

Life is change—growth is optional.

—Astro

Om Namah Shivaya: God dwells within you, as you.

—Sanskrit sutra

Our level of consciousness of universal laws determines our choices and how we live our lives.

—Theresa Marie

Hooray for the Universe For Making It All-Possible...

—Lee Whitman

*You've got to **Dance** like there's nobody watching,*

*You've got to **Love** like you've never been hurt.*

*You've got to **Sing** like there's nobody listening,*

*You've got to **Live** like it's Heaven on Earth.*

—based on the song "Come from the Heart"
by Kathy Mattea

The secret of Life...is to LIVE it.